BIG RIVER TO CROSS

Mississippi Life Today

BY BEN LUCIEN BURMAN

MISSISSIPPI

STEAMBOAT ROUND THE BEND

BLOW FOR A LANDING

BIG RIVER TO CROSS

Old Al .. *King of the River.*

BEN LUCIEN BURMAN

BIG RIVER
TO CROSS

Mississippi Life Today

Drawings by Alice Caddy

THE JOHN DAY COMPANY

NEW YORK

Manufactured in the United States of America
Van Rees Press, New York

FOR

BLANCHE COLTON WILLIAMS

AND

EDWARD J. O'BRIEN

*whose unselfishness and kindness have made life's
rivers run smoother for so many young writers
setting out on their literary voyages.*

ACKNOWLEDGMENTS

To all his friends on the Mississippi, captains and carpenters, pilots and pursers, lightkeepers and locktenders, dredgers and deckhands, snagboaters and shantymen, the writer once more wishes to express his deep-felt gratitude, and humbly hopes that these pages may bring some slight understanding of the river to the men and women who watch from the shore.

CONTENTS

INTRODUCTION

THE Mississippi River of the twentieth century and all of its tributaries had long been in need of an interpreter when Ben Lucien Burman appeared upon the horizon.

No one disputed that the Mississippi had long captivated, and continued to captivate, the average American mind. The enduring popularity of *Life On The Mississippi* was proof sufficient of that. But with every passing year the need for a new Mark Twain was more and more in evidence.

Travelers in the busy, modern world, as they whisked across the big river in railway cars and automobiles, consciously or unconsciously regretted their unseemly haste. They regretted their lack of acquaintance with the river of rivers that still cast a spell over their imaginations; they wondered whether sometime, somewhere an individual might not be found who would bridge the gap between today and yesterday and bring them to a knowledge of the great stream.

It was a problem that continued to be unsolved until the advent of Ben Lucien Burman.

The story of the author's life is fascinating; it is remarkable also as a tribute to the potency of the spell of the big river. But there is no place for details here. Let it suffice to say that in 1929 there came from Burman's pen a full length novel named, very simply, *Mississippi*. People read it, Hollywood filmed it, though in unrecognizable fashion, and the river, through Mr. Burman, was on the way to rediscovery.

In *Mississippi* one need proceed no farther than the first

few pages to read these phrases which so fitly express the feeling of the riverman toward the stream on which he floats: "River is a beautiful thing. More than that she's a kind of holy thing. Don't need to go to church when you're on the river."

"The river is practically a religion with this author," I remember remarking at the time. And so it is with all rivermen and all who love the river.

With his first novel, Mr. Burman, in popular parlance, arrived. His *Steamboat Round The Bend* followed, and, much changed like the first, was made into a motion picture with the talents of Will Rogers.

"This is such a book as Mark Twain would have relished and understood," wrote one reviewer when the novel first appeared.

"And it is such a book as the American people and people all over the world have been waiting for and will understand as well," the critic might have added.

In 1938 Mr. Burman presented *Blow For A Landing*. Said one famous critic: "It has the quality of universality that will make it, I believe, one of the longest lived and best loved among novels of America, old or new." It is the author's favorite of his novels, on which he labored five years; at a time when fine Southern books were everywhere it won the Southern Author's Award as the most distinguished Southern book of the year. Of it a literature professor at Harvard, Mr. Burman's alma mater, wrote that it has an "I-wanna-be-lazy flavor." And there again one obtains an insight into this author's appeal to people who, caught in the hurrying surge of the twentieth century, glory in discovering that the river is still just drifting slowly on its way;

that upon it, immune from gas, water, and light bills, and income tax reports, are thousands of people leading lives of sheer serenity.

Mississippi, Steamboat Round The Bend, and *Blow For A Landing* held up mirrors of contemporary life the average person had never dreamed could still exist in the bustling, hustling America of today. But having read these books it has not escaped them that the river was and is one of the fundamentals in making and keeping the United States the home of the individualist. Few perhaps realize that one of the wells from which Abraham Lincoln dipped deep for his insight into life and his ability to cope calmly with emergencies was the river. It is difficult to estimate the importance in the development of Lincoln's character of his days as a flatboater and later as a steamboat man upon the Ohio and the Mississippi.

It is because they reveal this individualistic life of the riverman that the two remaining steamboats of old-time flavor still carrying passengers between Pittsburgh, the Twin Cities, and New Orleans are at times compelled to turn away many prospective patrons. And there is perhaps another reason as well. It is the slow ways of the lazy old paddling sternwheeler that today seem new and startling; it is the high-powered automobiles and the glistening streamliners that are beginning to pall and grow commonplace.

All of these truths of the river were discerned, albeit somewhat hazily at first, a good twenty years ago by Mr. Burman. Even then he saw them clearly enough to leave his newspaper work in New York, and return to Covington, in Kentucky, where he had grown up along the banks of the Ohio. At first he merely sat at the water's edge and watched the remaining steamboats, chiefly towboats pushing barges. Then he did the natural thing and followed the river, downstream, to the lower country. There he found the *Tennessee Belle*. He boarded her and won the friendship of Capt. Dick Dicharry; he admired the Captain's prodigious effort, still successful, to run a nineteenth-century river packet in an era of freight trains, motor trucks, and airplanes.

Mr. Burman made many trips from New Orleans up the big river on the *Tennessee Belle* and the other vessels of the lower river. He stopped at the way landings and loafed with the river folk; he took his daily five grains of quinine to live with the inhabitants of the malarial swamps.

Were there anything not genuine in Ben Lucien Burman's writings about the river and river folk I should probably have been the first to notice. I was formerly a pilot; my own opportunities to ride on the river, and to tarry in the remote hamlets on the banks have been constant for thirty years. Like other rivermen I even indulged in dreams of myself interpreting the river. But I was busy, always too busy. Ben Lucien Burman found the time.

On the river there are many wistful individuals. All of them, with their dreams and aspirations, are known and understood by Mr. Burman, who, coupled with his great genius as a writer, is a man of infinite patience and sympathy as well. He loves the river people; he is one with them. He as no other man in America knows them, shantyboater and steamboater alike. At times writing in a vein almost mystic, he wins at once the interest of his readers who revel in discovering that America still has its frontiers.

Now Ben Lucien Burman has written a purely descriptive book about the Mississippi as it is today, and I am here, proudly, to pronounce it genuine. In *Big River to Cross* the author brings the river and its men and women to life.

No novice could do this; Mr. Burman himself could not have done it ten or fifteen years ago before he had fully succumbed to the river's spell and had begun to live so much of his life upon it.

Mr. Burman knows the steamboat. He is an expert on such details as the difference between the fantail on the stern and the fans that cool the passengers up in the cabin. The rivermen love their steamboats and appreciate his understanding. They open their hearts and their minds to him. Whether they work on packet, towboat, light tender, or dredge, he has visited them all. And there is real elation among the crew, from captain to the lowliest deck hand, when Mr. Burman walks aboard.

"Maybe our boat will be in a book," they say. "Maybe we'll even get our names into print."

But Mr. Burman seems not to hear. It is not of self-conscious rivermen that he writes. He only begins to notice when men are off their guard and doing their steamboating subconsciously. Show him something, tell him something, and the chances it will appear in a Burman book are remote. But travel with him on the river, as I have done, and read the next volume. Suddenly the central theme of some chapter will come back to his fellow voyager as a vividly remembered experience.

"Big River to Cross." So thought Eads when he flung his great bridge over it at St. Louis. But it is an even bigger river to have lived upon, to have understood, to have interpreted.

Mr. Burman has written three novels. Now, for a fourth time, without trappings or tinsel, he has laid bare for Americans the very soul of the great river that Thomas Jefferson pridefully secured in its entirety for the young republic.

Here in his first factual book about his beloved Mississippi, the author tells us as only he can about the sprawling stream and its kaleidoscopic moods and vagaries that are, after all, permanent through the ages.

Here, in *Big River to Cross*, the Mississippi meets a great and understanding mind, the mind of Ben Lucien Burman.

CAPTAIN DONALD T. WRIGHT

Editor, the *Waterways Journal*

St. Louis, Missouri

March 10th, 1940

Riverman

I

STEAMBOAT

ON certain late afternoons, say the negro roustabouts, when the sun is sinking toward the horizon, and the water becomes a mysterious purple, there will rise up before a steamboat a glistening alligator of a vastness beyond description, carrying in one of his scaly paws a great pipe of tobacco, and bearing on his enormous head a shiny golden crown.

For a moment this bizarre creature will remain before the vessel, surveying the river and the sandbars and the cypress swamps beyond, then will flap his tail lazily, and disappear beneath the surface, to sink back into the mud of the bottom from which he arose. And the roustabouts aboard the steamboat will shudder, and will touch their good luck charms, or if churchly negroes will breathe a prayer; for they have seen Old Al, the River King.

At another time, in the cotton season, when the negroes have been toiling without ceasing as the vessel moves from plantation to plantation, picking up at each landing a new mountain of cotton bales, the chance traveler will see a negro furtively drop some tobacco over the railing into the yellow water. The negro is not wasting his tobacco; this is a ritual of sacrifice, to induce Old Al, the monarch, to smoke the kingly pipe he is always carrying. For when Old Al smokes his pipe there comes a thick fog as the fumes rise through the water; the boat can no longer travel, and the roustabout may rest.

It is a vast kingdom over which Old Al extends his rule, a kingdom where life has changed little with the passing of the years. I have sat on the waterfront of a sleepy little town and watched a steamboat moving down the river, her tall stacks towering into the sky and pouring forth clouds of smoke like a rushing tornado; if the day was warm and dreamy, with green dragonflies floating drowsily about my head, it was easy to believe that this was not reality, but that by some curious metamorphosis I had drifted back into the days of the War between the States. For running water, and the creatures which float upon it, are part of the basic forces of nature, immutable in the scheme of the universe, like light and darkness, and life and death. Which is the reason why the Mississippi today is a sanctuary for those weary of a mechanical world where the machine is master and man its beaten slave: it is a delight to the eye and to the ear, a treasury of beauty and rich humanity.

An automobile is the giddy creature of a nerve-racked

world, fit only to speed its owner off to a sanitarium that he may recover from the frenzy it has helped induce. An automobile will jolt the traveler from New Orleans to Greenville, Mississippi, in perhaps eight or nine hours. On a steamboat the round trip between the same two points may require two weeks. For a steamboat is of a courtly, gentle breed, who knows that not in fever but in leisure and grace and philosophic calm lies the secret of a happy life. When a packet boat saw an old negro waving a battered hat on the shore, she stopped to take him aboard, with his woebegone dog and his fragment of a stove; if she saw a fire burning at night along the edge of a piney wood, she steamed carefully toward it and watched till the grizzled farmer standing there had driven his grunting pigs up the gangplank.

Whatever changes may have come upon the towns along the shore, the river remains basically as it was in the olden days, beautiful, cruel, fascinating, terrible, always unpredictable. I have seen huge sandbars form, ten miles long and a mile wide, only to disappear overnight in some sweeping yellow onrush. There are still few settlements in the valley which can be sure that when a raging flood has reached its height, a vast section of the city will not be swept into the water; many a thriving river town may wonder, when the flood subsides, whether it will be the ghost of an inland city twenty miles from the stream, because Old Al has chosen this moment to cut through a bend.

It is this temperamental, almost demoniac quality, which has given the steamboating of the past and the steamboating of today so much of its picturesqueness. For there can be no mechanical rules for piloting a boat in a channel that may cease to exist before the rising of tomorrow's sun.

There were colorful steamboatmen in the olden days, characters like the tempestuous Captain Leathers, who, when he saw a passenger whittling at the railing of his finest boat, whipped out a knife and began slashing at the passenger's clothing; and when the passenger remonstrated that the captain was cutting his coat, replied fierily: "Yes sir. Damn it, sir. You're cutting my boat."

But there are characters to equal him today. There are figures like Captain Barney, who every evening before supper lowers a tin bucket into the muddy river, and, when it is filled, drinks the thick brown fluid until every drop has vanished. "Keeps my health a-going good," he drawls lazily. "It's this here filtering and all these fancy fixings they do to the water that causes all the sickness there is nowadays. Just takes all the strength out of it."

And on the same boat there is Blue Johnny, an engineer noted for his tippling, who early in the morning goes to his chief and declares: "Captain, give me the orders for everything you want me to do the rest of the day, 'cause I'm going to get drunk in an hour, and then I won't be able to understand 'em." Given the orders, he remembers them in his Bacchanalian depths, and executes each one with faithfulness and precision, a phenomenon which might cause a psychologist to wonder.

There is a wide variety of craft over which Old Al extends his sway: the rare packet boat, direct descendant of the *Natchez* and the *Robt. E. Lee;* the Government dredges which keep the channel clear of mud and the lighthouse boats that bring supplies for the lamps high on odd-shaped standards along the shore; the towboats, those valiant workers of the river, found wherever the yellow water flows, always puffing laboriously behind their great barges, and so numerous today they are carrying more freight than at any time in the river's colorful history.

The size of the boats is varied as their natures. It may be some huge vessel of a barge line which legend says can move simultaneously all the railroad cars in a vast freight yard; it may be some tiny, battered craft, like one boat I know whose captain is said to keep a rowboat floating inside the leaky hull in order that the carpenter may row back and forth and patch the breaks more easily.

But wherever the boat and whatever its type; though it may be a sleek new vessel just from the shipyards, boasting

The Tennessee Belle

a radio, and shining Diesel engines, and even that abomination of the riverman, the twin screws of an ocean liner, the pilot house, which is the heart of the steamboat, remains the same as in the olden days, its problems identical.

Many years ago I shipped as cub pilot under one of the most famous steersmen on the Mississippi. I shall never forget that first trip through the darkness; the miraculous way in which the pilot, casually glancing down the dark water, turned the wheel and sent the vessel toward the shore. A moment later, as accurately as though it were an automobile moving into the driveway of a bright-lighted filling station, the boat landed at a minute gap in the endless line of willows. A score of muddy mules came stamping aboard, dragging the clanking machinery of a levee camp behind them. I marveled then how the shadow of a distant clump of cottonwoods, the dim shape of a far-off oak tree, was to that pilot as a flaming beacon, when to the ordinary eye the shadow and the shape were repeated a thousand times in the black horizon.

And though I have been on the river many years since, and have often, in the feeble way of a cub, guided a steamboat along its course, I continue to marvel. For just as in Twain's time, the pilot must know all the stream's fantastic vagaries: how it is a far different river on the trip going down than when he came up it only three days before. If he does not proceed with incredible care, the boat will go aground on a new reef suddenly formed along Paddy Hen or strike a new snag at Hard Times Light that will pierce the hull like a child's knife thrust into a Christmas drum.

Piloting is difficult on ordinary occasions. But it is fog which requires from the steersman extraordinary, almost superhuman qualities. The good fog pilot is the pilot that ties up his boat, runs the river proverb. But at times the vessel must leave the wharf on some urgent errand, or Old Al suddenly smokes his pipe and the gray fog sweeps down in a section of the river where mooring the craft is impossible. It is these occasions which have given rise to so much of the Mississippi's rich folklore. I know steersmen, who, legend says, can blow the whistle in a fog, and merely by listening to the echo, tell whether they are in front of a cliff, a tree, a sandbar, a house, or even a double house. I have heard the story of Captain Barney, whose course ran along dangerous shoal water often covered with a blinding fog. But near by there lived a farmer with a keen-witted dog, devoted to Captain Barney and the other steamboatmen. Whenever the vessel neared the reef in the mist, Captain Barney had merely to ring the bell as a signal. The dog would bark loudly in answer. The pilot, thus told of his location, could go blithely on his way.

But tragedy came at last. One night, during a foggy blackness unparalleled in the memory of rivermen, Captain Barney approached the shoal and rang the bell as usual. No answering bark came from the distance. Some warning instinct troubled him, and he rang again. Still there was no response. He hesitated, then at last, certain that his four-legged friend would not fail him, drove the boat ahead. A moment later the vessel was breaking up on the rocks. The dog had died the night before.

I have heard how Captain Barney, trapped one night in another dense fog, ordered his mate to go ashore and slice off some bark from the shadowy trees to which the boat had drifted. Captain Barney studied the woody fiber a moment, then nodded sagely.

"I know them trees," he grunted. "Them's the cottonwoods

on John Sizemore's place. The cottonwoods down near the stable. We're all right now. Full speed ahead."

I have listened to the tales of how the graceful cranes are the Samaritans of the river. The cranes, as every Mississippi dweller knows, are old steamboatmen, reincarnated as the long white birds so that they may stand all day with their feet in the water and watch the paddlewheels churn foamily past. In a fog, they are the snag hunters for their old associates. Slowly they fly ahead of the boat to a snag that would pierce its bottom, rest there until assured the pilot has seen the peril, and then fly gravely on to the next obstruction; until by this laborious procedure, the steersman at length can bring his vessel safely into harbor.

"Plenty of times I've had them cranes take me home," says Captain Barney. "Mile after mile."

Steamboaters form a close-knit fraternity, with an amiable sufferance of the dweller on the land. But wherever men live and work in close association there spring up feuds arising from the occupation and the basic perversity of humankind. The feuds on the river today as in the past, have a particular zest and savor. There is the constant feud between the pilot and the engineer. When the landing is bad the pilot blames the engineer for his slowness in responding to a signal; but the engineer, sweating at his throttle, curses only the steersman's clumsiness. Blue Johnny was working once with a pilot noted for his temperamental steering. The vessel tied up at the wharf of a little town; the crew donned their Sunday clothes and began trooping ashore for a few hours' holiday. But Blue Johnny did not join them. Instead he began dashing frantically about the engine room, like an animal seized by some strange fit, now sending the engines into half speed, now suddenly throwing them into reverse, then frantically pulling the levers forward once more in a giddy full speed ahead.

The captain of the vessel, hastily summoned, looked on in alarm.

"What you doing, Johnny?" he demanded. "You going crazy?"

Blue Johnny shook his head in angry negation. With a grease-spattered hand he threw the engines into a wild reverse again. "Ain't doing nothing," he exploded. "Just trying to catch up with all them signals that blankety-blank pilot give me so I can be finished with 'em before we get to the next landing."

But surpassing all river feuds is the conflict between steam-

boater and shantyman. It began when the first steamboat paddlewheel went churning up the stream and sent the nearby shantyboats into a frenzied dance, causing dishes to crash from shanty walls and frying pans of bacon to fly wildly from their stoves. It continues today with all its earlier bitterness. The kindly pilot will slow down when he passes a shantyboat, so that the waves will not disturb the frail craft. But at times the more mirthful-minded steersman will race as he draws near, and watch with delight as the shanty bobs up and down in the water. The tattered proprietor who has been sitting on his porch must cling desperately to a pillar to save himself from drowning. After such an occasion, when the steamboat next voyages down the river, the shantyman may take down his long rifle and shoot through the pilot house window. The bullet may merely break the glass. But since every shantyman is expert as an Indian with his rifle, the bullet is likely to find a residence in the steersman's shoulder.

I stood on the sunbaked wharf at Greenville one afternoon, gravely discussing the problem with a wistful-faced shantyman who was watching the roustabouts unload the steamboat from which I had descended. "Them people on the *Tennessee Belle* is nice people," he murmured, as he bit thoughtfully into the plug of tobacco I had brought him. "They'll always slow down when they see a shantyboat, so it don't do no rocking. But there's some pilots, seems like, just wants to torment 'em every time they can. I knowed a mighty fine pilot on a boat once used to tie a newspaper on a stick and throw it out for me and my pardner to catch. I ain't got no book reading, but my pardner had, and he'd read 'em and tell me what was a-going on away up North and them places. And then they got a new pilot. He throwed out the paper on the stick the same way. But when we rowed out to get it, it was wrote in what they call the Germany language or some funny kind of talking. He couldn't read it no-ways. And the pilot just stood there watching and busting his sides a-laughing. It ain't right to treat nobody thataway."

His face grew sad. "And just last week I lost a mighty fine picture account of a steamboat rocking. It was a wonderful picture. Showed Jesus coming into Jerusalem on a donkey. There was mighty fine mother of pearl on her. Had a angel with wings made of real butterflies, and one little nigger with real hair on him."

He called to a dilapidated dog who was disputing with a fat pig the ownership of some potatoes spilled on the wharf, and chewed his tobacco in thought again. "It's like this about them kind of pilots," he said. "You warn 'em twice to slow down. You give 'em fair warning twice. And the third time, if they don't slow down, it's according to the law to shoot 'em."

Steamboat racing, too, still occasions its feuds, but here, though feeling waxes bitter, there are no rifles. Racing is forbidden by the Government because of the succession of disasters that marked its history. But the love of a race is an ancient human attribute, whether it be vice or virtue, and the crews of boats whose speed is much the same sometimes forget the laws made by a dusty office in far-off Washington. For measured in terms of excitement, even a horse race by comparison seems colorless and dull. In the steamboat race, the passenger is no mere spectator; he shares all the thrills of the jockey as well, for he is riding the racer.

Peer of all races on the river was the race between the *Natchez* and the *Robt. E. Lee.* There has long been a legend that the crew of the *Natchez* took all the fanciest hams that hung in the cook's galley for the passengers, and burnt them in the fire-boxes to make more steam for the engines. Wrinkled old negroes, all along the course of the vessel, smacked their lips as a rich fragrance drifted out on the water and they murmured: "Ain't that wonderful frying ham? Ain't that sure wonderful ham?"

The crew of the *Natchez* did burn ham. But the meat did not come from the boat's stores. It was a supply of condemned hams donated for the purpose by the merchants of Natchez.

There is another colorful legend: the reason why the *Natchez* lost the race. The *Natchez,* an old riverman once told me, was steaming far ahead, and the prize seemed hers to a certainty; the exultant crew began to celebrate their victory. Suddenly, at the height of their jollity, a dismal thought occurred to one of the pilots, and continued to haunt him like a ghost at the feast: if the *Natchez* won, the name of the beloved *Robt. E. Lee* would be associated with defeat. He kept silence for a while, then communicated his fears to his companions. Instantly the merriment ceased. A council was held, and the matter gravely debated. The decision was made at last: for the sake of the great general, they must lose the race. The plan was quickly carried into execution. The boat swung to the shore, and hid deep in a cove. For hours she lay there, lost to the sight of any river travelers, waiting patiently, stoically, until the *Robt. E. Lee* roared past and went steaming into glory.

The most common type of riverboat today is the stern-wheeler, with paddles churning busily at her back in a white circle of spray like an old lady's bustle. As in the olden days, their cargoes are a catalogue of the industries they border. The greater part of the freight is concentrated on the larger rivers, like the Mississippi and the Ohio and the smoke-fringed Monongahela. But there is a lesser steamboating up the smaller tributaries also termed navigable by the Government, a classification which a cursing captain grounded on a sandbar is sometimes apt to question. For when a vessel ventures up such a stream, the voyage may become a veritable Odyssey. Here the stranded captain may not be able to free his vessel in a day, a week, or even a month; if he escapes the snags he may be compelled to jump for his life as the pilot house is torn away by the bough of a tree. And the natives along the banks, unaccustomed to steamboatmen, may be more difficult than the natural obstacles. Once Captain Barney took his boat into one of the streams that rises in the Ozarks to bring out a barge load of cotton and after voyaging a few miles found his way blocked by one of those curious ferries so characteristic of the lower valley. A steel cable was stretched from a tree on one shore to a tree on the other; the ferryman by means of a windlass pulled the craft laboriously from side to side. The steel cable at the moment was stretched above the water so that any traffic on the stream was impossible. Politely Captain Barney, as was usual, requested that the ferryman lower the wire so that his vessel might move past. The ferryman, a towering individual who hated all steamboatmen because of a fancied injury twenty years before, paid no attention.

Captain Barney at last turned angrily to his mate. "Get a rouster to cut the cable damn quick," he commanded.

A negro shuffled forward with an axe.

Suddenly the boat's carpenter, a native of the region, who had just learned of the altercation, came running in panic. "For God's sake, Captain, don't cut it!" he shouted. "This here ferry keeper's the toughest man in the valley. He's got four brothers scattered all the way up the river and we've got to pass 'em all four. Nobody here 'd ever get back alive. 'Cause him and his brothers is the best shots in Arkansas."

Captain Dick had a similar adventure. The chief of the army enlistment bureau in New Orleans named him an honorary recruiting officer, and in token of the appointment gave him a large recruiting flag. Proudly Captain Dick flew the banner over the pilot house of his *Tennessee Belle*. All went well until he was called to take the boat up a swampy

bayou famed for its moonshiners. He reached the stream, and was rounding the first of the moss-hung cypresses that formed its boundaries, when a bullet crashed through the pilot house window. In a moment there was pandemonium; rifles cracked and bullets whistled everywhere.

The moonshiners had seen Captain Dick's new flag, and decided he was a revenue officer.

The flag came down.

The Mississippi sternwheeler is flat-bottomed as a packing crate—to which some sacrilegious land dwellers have likened its entire structure—and can move in the incredible depth of three and a half feet of water. But at times, even this slight depth may be lacking. And it is in such a region, where the pilot fears he may be trapped in the stream's muddy embrace, that the rivermen are actors in what is perhaps the most colorful scene on the Mississippi.

I was standing watch not long ago in the dark pilot house of the *Belle,* looking at the channel lights that shone brilliantly through the blackness, while the sky hung so close the fretted tops of the smokestacks seemed at each instant to scoop out great segments of the stars. Suddenly the pilot, smoking a cigar near me, blew a short summoning blast of the whistle.

"She's low tonight," he declared thoughtfully. "I'm going to take soundings."

A moment later a giant negro clad in burlap rags and answering to the name of Chattanooga Jack appeared on the bow and picked up the measuring line; a little negro called Bantam took a post just below the pilot house.

The black giant at the prow tossed the line and quickly drew it toward him, then threw back his glistening head.

"O Mark F-o-u-r!" he chanted in a voice poignant with melancholy. "O Mark F-o-u-r!"

Bantam, at the pilot house, turned his twisted little body to listen. Then his head too, bent sharply backward, and from his throat there came an echoing call, in a sobbing tremolo: "O Mark F-o-u-r! O Mark F-o-u-r!"

The pilot turned to me in the blackness. "Four fathoms. Plenty of water for a minute," he said quietly.

The giant negro at the prow swung the lead again. "Quarter Less Three," he chanted. "Quarter Less Three."

"Quarter Less Three," echoed Bantam at the pilot house, in his throbbing voice like a violin string about to break. "O Quarter Less Three."

"Sixteen and a half feet," announced the pilot. He offered me a cigar.

I smoked with him in silence, while the boat moved on slowly. In troubled succession there came the calls, "Half Twain," "Mark Twain," "Quarter Less Twain," with always their quavering echo. Suddenly there came a sharp cry, "Five feet!"

Before the words were finished, the pilot gave the bell cord a violent jerk. The paddlewheel churned whitely. There was a harsh grinding along the bottom. The vessel shuddered, and seemed to halt. The paddlewheel churned in desperation. Great foaming crescents poured from its huge blades. The boat shivered like a frightened animal, and was free again.

"Close one," muttered Captain Dick, who had come up from the shadows.

The shoal ended. The croaking of the frogs in the willows grew fainter as the shore glided swiftly away. The twisted little negro joined the burlapped giant below. They started to shuffle across the deck.

Captain Dick called after them. "Good singing, boys. Tell the cook to give you what you want to eat."

He turned to me as they hurried off gaily. "Won't have a leadsman isn't a good singer. Rather lose my boat."

The vessel steamed into the starry blackness.

But it is not all picturesqueness which makes up the life of the steamboat man. For Old Al is ever ready with some new grim trick; in an instant tranquillity may change to stark tragedy. I have stood on a vessel moored to the bank in the quietest water, when without warning some mysterious current seized the hull, and twisted it violently. The heavy boom stretching above me to support the gangplank, smashed into a tree, and fell a few feet from my head, hurling the mate and a score of shouting negroes into the water. I have been a cub beside the pilot when a hurricane blew up from the Gulf, and have watched the vessel sweep out of control, while the pilot house, attached only by frail guy wires, quivered and a thousand times seemed about to topple into the swirling water. I have been on a steamboat in the floods that sweep down the valley till the earth for miles is only a gray memory, and have watched the pilot, already exhausted from his labors, cheerfully take his vessel through new flood waters threatening each instant to overwhelm him, that he might bring food to the hungry and life to the drowning.

Like the sailor, the mountaineer, or any of those sturdy souls whose lives are spent at the mercy of the inconstant elements, the riverman is a supreme fatalist. Each time he takes his vessel through a rain-swollen eddy and hears its ominous lapping against the hull; each time the lightning flashes in the distance and he drives his boat into a clump of half-submerged trees along the shore so that the towering hulk may have a feeble shelter from the oncoming storm, he knows well that this adventure may be his last. But he is a cheerful fatalist, as brave a figure as has voyaged the waters of the earth, laughing in the face of the fate that destroys him, loyal to his boat literally to the death—and beyond death.

As long as the surging yellow waters roll past the levees and the channel lights, I shall think of the final act of a pilot whom it was my good fortune to have as a teacher and a friend. Alone late at night in the pilot house, with the boat far out in a treacherous stretch of the river, he was suddenly seized with a fatal stroke. Knowing the vessel's peril as death swept swiftly down upon him, with a fierce effort he reached out his foot and pressed the whistle treadle, so that as life ceased and he fell forward, the weight of his body started the whistle blowing. Even in death his foot remained there, keeping the whistle at full blast, until someone came to take the wheel he could guard no more. And thus he saved the vessel and its crew from destruction.

Let the traveler who demands for his pleasure only the spectacular landscapes of the Alps and the Sierras, and all the other sweeping panoramas of nature in her giant moods, keep far from the river. He will not find these here. But if he has within him the faintest spark of that poetry with which almost every dweller on this troubled sphere is blessed, he will find a beauty, a soft tranquillity, from which ever after there is no escaping. He will know the joy of watching a white prow glide across a cloud-studded sky; he will know the charm of rounding green bend on bend where negroes labor in the snowy fields of cotton and a grizzled shantyman sits beneath the willows, catching his supper with a fishing line. He will know the sad beauty of the river night: the melancholy sighing of the smokestacks and the hushed chanting of the roustabouts as in accompaniment; the distant hooting of the owl and the mournful cry of the whippoorwill. While the boat moves steadily along an endless line of trees through a ghostly world that time and life have forgotten.

I have not read what epitaph lies carved on the gravestone of my friend who died at the wheel. I am not much given to cemeteries. But there should be written only these simple words: "He loved a steamboat."

And those who have watched the waves of a paddlewheel sweep out whitely beneath them to beat against the green willowed shore, will know—and understand.

II

ROUSTABOUT

FROM the time when the United States first became a nation, there have always been in the rich pageant of its history certain typical figures who evoke a whole era. A painting of a stern-browed Puritan walking grimly past the village church instantly calls up all the troubled

years of the founding of New England, with its witch burn-
ers and its Indians. The picture of a weary, unshaven figure
sitting behind his horses on the seat of a covered wagon at
once recalls all the dangers and the trials of the Western pioneers. The view of a lean individual standing with his rifle
beside the porch of his bleak log cabin conjures up all the
moonshine stills and the bitter feud killings of the Kentucky
mountaineers. And of all these figures, there is none more
symbolic than the negro steamboat deck hand, the Mississippi roustabout.

To the shopgirl in Seattle or the stately cliff dweller on
New York's Park Avenue, to the Parisian strolling in the
Champs Elysées or the Italian sipping his Espresso at
the Piazza Santa Lucia in Naples, the mere mention of the
roustabout instantly summons up visions of racing steamboats with great flames leaping from their stacks, and pictures of broad-hatted gamblers with pistols at their belts
defrauding wealthy planters from New Orleans. For to those
remote from the Mississippi, and to many near it as well, the
roustabout was better known than any other part of a steamboat, being considered a sort of colorful ornament, like the
boat's gilded cotton bale, with no duties except to sit in the
sun playing a mellow banjo. The gamblers have gone now,
with the planters and the pistols. But the roustabout remains—little changed with time. He still dresses in the same
picturesque fashion, a piece of burlap for a shirt, and a fragment of a lady's hat with a few artificial grapes still clinging
to the brim. At night he will sit on the prow as the boat
steams on in the moonlight and chant plaintively:

"Captain, Captain, is your money come?
I jest wants to know, 'cause I wants to borrow some."

But in one respect the shopgirl in Seattle and the Italian at his café in Naples were wrong; the roustabout is not an ornament. He is as vital a part of a steamboat as the engines or the paddle wheel. He is the steamboat man of all work: a combination stevedore and fourth-class sailor. If the boat is swinging into shore for a landing, and a rope must be thrown swiftly around a tree stump to arrest the vessel's course, it is the roustabout who tosses the line; if a tarpaulin blows free in a hurricane, it is the roustabout who goes out in the fury of the wind and lashes the cover down again. Though he may have been working for twenty-four hours rolling great bales of cotton onto the boat, and a new load unexpectedly arrives for hurried transport down the river, it is the roustabout who must bring the bales aboard. He groans a moment, stretches his weary limbs, then grins, and chanting a cotton-rolling song, starts striding up the gangplank. He must carry coal for the fireman or be ready to leap into the water and dig the boat free if she is aground. He must go out on the tow to untangle a line that has fouled, at the risk of having his foot cut off by a twisting rope or being crushed to death between the barges. So broken is his rest that when a roustabout I knew died, his black friends assured me the reason given by the doctors was that he was five years behind in his sleep.

The roustabout is generally a superb physical specimen, the pick of his race, with a resistance to injury that is sometimes astounding. I was on the *Tennessee Belle* with my friend Captain Dick one hot summer night at Natchez when Half Dollar, a lanky, amiable roustabout was attacked with a razor by a negro hiding in the darkness of the bank. Before Half Dollar could resist, he had been so desperately wounded the doctors at the hospital to which the captain had rushed him, abandoned all hope of saving his life. The *Belle* continued on her journey to Greenville, with all the crew certain that poor Half Dollar was dead. Five days later the vessel returned to Natchez and began to unload her cargo. Suddenly the roustabouts ceased their labor, and grew pale. A lanky figure was moving down the hill. It was Half Dollar. Slowly he walked up the gangplank and made his way to Captain Dick, standing at the bow. His face was thin, ema- ciated, and his step a little unsteady; the unevenness of his clothing betrayed the thick bandages round his body. But his voice when he spoke was determined.

"Captain Dick, I jest got terrible tired in that there hos- pital," he declared. "Can't see the river, or hear the steam- boats, or nothing. So I come down to ask you to give me back my job."

It is this almost superhuman strength that makes the rousta- bout at once the envy and the terror of his fellows on the shore. The roustabout in his youth was generally a planta- tion negro. But he has long forgotten the days when he left his bandanaed mother and a rickety horse in the cotton patch to take his first job on a steamboat. He has nothing now but scorn for the poor farm negro—and the sophisti- cated poolroom negro of the city as well. He steals the land negro's girl or his wife without compunction. When he doffs his tatters and puts on the purple-striped suit he has pur- chased for ten times its value from some shrewd merchant in a country town, he is a dashing Don Juan whom no negress can resist.

His scorn for the shore negro does not cease even when the other has come to his aid. Sometimes when in an emer- gency the roustabouts had been toiling for thirty-six hours without respite, I have seen a steamboat captain hire several

score land negroes to help them at their labor. On each occasion, though the roustabouts were at the point of exhaustion, their pride of craft was so intense, they tried every means to bring about the discharge of their unwanted assistants, trampling on the others' feet when they were nearing the water so that the huge bale of cotton they were carrying would escape from their inexpert cotton hooks and fall into the river. The scorn of the roustabout extends even to the other negroes on the boat, the cookhouse negroes, generally a quieter, softer breed, whom he considers as dandies without strength and fit only to do the work of women.

Yet with all his Herculean powers and his fierceness in battle, he is like a friendly child in his nature, and in dealing with his white masters has a gentleness and tact that is remarkable. I know a little roustabout named Piece O' Man, who is acting as night watchman on a vessel, and is compelled to call the crew early in the morning. Worried, because like all sleepers they bitterly resented being awakened, for weeks Piece O' Man pondered over a remedy. And at last inspiration came to aid him. Now as the hour of the captain or the mate approaches, he opens the door of the cabin, steps quietly inside, and standing by the sleeper's bed, begins to execute an ingratiating, comical dance that grows faster and faster as the drowsy figure before him sits up and rubs his eyes. At the same time he begins to sing in a curious jargon a little tune, repeated over and over:

"The old cow died at the fork of the branch.
Jaybird died of the measles.
Here come Mr. Rabbit with a fiddle on his back.
Going home to Jesus."

"Seems like they's never mad now when I gits 'em up," he declares gravely. "They never swears or throws shoes or nothing. I reckon it's the Jesus in the song keeps 'em a-feeling good."

The roustabout is like a child in most of his pleasures. A huge horse head set on a ring, with imitation emeralds for its eyes and a glaring ruby for its lips, or perhaps a watch where two negroes battle with their fists and feet at each swing of the balance wheel: these are enough to send him into ecstasies. Like a child, he makes a pet of anything which is at hand, and spends a large portion of his scanty income buying it presents. There is a rat living down in the hold of a boat I know which the roustabouts have tamed and named Mr. Wingfield, because he can travel so fast; to bring Mr. Wingfield or his devoted wife Bunny Bee some tidbit from the cookhouse, the roustabouts would gladly risk their jobs and their lives. Where there is a pet pig on a boat, they will keep it scrubbed immaculate, constantly buying a new collar of blue baby ribbon to tie about its neck; at night they never stretch out on their beds of sugar sacks without first making sure that the softest place is left vacant for their porcine friend to snuggle at their sides.

Their imaginations are likewise childish and delightful; they are always living in a world of wonder. On a rainy night, as the boat slips dreamily past the endless cypress swamps, Piece O' Man will tell you the story of his friend Big Black.

"Big Black was a Greenville nigger a-rousting on the *Tennessee Belle*," he declares. "But he got tired of the river and went on one of them ships that goes out of New Orleans to the sea. The weather kept getting hotter and hotter. And the mate seen him looking at the water and said, 'Don't you go in swimming, Big Black.' He didn't tell him why, though, and one day, when it was terrible hot, Big Black jumped in the ocean. And in a minute, a lot of them Her-girls, that's half women, half fish, grabbed him and pulled him down to the bottom. They sit him up on a big rock, and then they all yelled at him: 'Greenville Nigger, do you like fish?'

"Big Black was awful scared, and he didn't know what to answer. But he'd been getting too much catfish at Greenville, so he says mighty quiet: 'If it's something to eat you wants to give me, if you'll please 'scuse me, I'd mighty like some pork chops or a nice chicken wing. I jest hates fish.' And then all them Her-girls clapped their hands. 'If you'd a-said you liked fish, we'd a-throwed you to the sharks,' they told him. 'You're the prettiest man we sure ever seen. We're going to make you our king.' And they swum in with a big gold throne. He was their king for a mighty long time. Twice every year he used to go back to Greenville, and give his mammy and pappy all the gold money they could carry and the finest pearls in the sea. But once he walked in the house, and there was a can of canned salmon laying on the table. He never come back no more."

Piece O' Man will also tell you why the otherwise mild deer suddenly goes into a frenzy when it sees a turtle on the bank, and crushes the shell to bits with fierce blows of its hoofs. The turtle and the deer once had a race in the fashion of the more famous contest between the hare and the tortoise; the deer, losing through overconfidence, vowed vengeance that he has not forgotten to this day.

Even when some happening is a fact actually within the roustabout's own experience, it becomes transfigured. My friend Chicken, so nicknamed because of his curious squeaky voice that sounds a little like the clucking of a hen, once left the *Tennessee Belle* on a visit to a city in the North, and saw there a giant policeman mounted on a beautiful horse. "I wasn't doing nothing," Chicken relates. "Jest a-looking, when they come running after me. I started going down the street, and I figured they sure wasn't going to catch me, 'cause when I runs from a policeman, I runs. But all of a sudden this here policeman jumped down from that horse, and he come one way round the block to head me off, and the horse run round the other. It was the horse that got me. Jest pushed me into a doorway, and stood there kind of laughing his head off for a minute. And then he took my coat in his teeth, and held me till the policeman come. It ain't right to have no horse like a man thataway."

And there is Chicken's famous adventure with royalty. Chicken was a patriot, and after America's entrance in the World War, left the river to sign as deck hand on the first mule transport voyaging to England. "It was a terrible trip," he will tell you. "But after a while we seen London, and the mate come down to where we was working and yelled out: 'Everybody git yourself shaved up, and put yourself on a nice clean shirt. 'Cause the King of England's coming down to meet you, and he's going to give you a basket of fruit.'

"We come into the harbor, and sure enough there the King was, a-waiting on the bank. He was a big, fine-looking man, kind of like Captain Dick, with a gold crown on his head so big they had a couple of people standing by him to push it back when it got to slipping. He was holding a big basket of fruit in his hands. And he give each of us a orange, a apple, and a banana. He kept me there on the bank a-talking a couple of hours, and I seen them fellows that pushed the crown gitting awful mad, so I said I'd better be going. But he shook his head. 'Don't you go,' he told me. 'I want to keep you with me all the time. I ain't never seen a Creole black man before.' Course I told him right away I couldn't. 'Cause I knowed Captain Dick 'd git mighty mad if I stayed away from the *Belle*."

The roustabout has the child's carefree attitude toward the future: the problems of tomorrow are matters with which he has no concern. The result is that he is one of the world's most prodigal spendthrifts. In five minutes he will be rid of the pay he has labored for weeks accumulating. And as he is a spendthrift, so is he also one of the world's most inveterate gamblers. Gambling to the roustabout is more than mere relaxation; it is a second occupation, almost as important a part of steamboating as wheeling coal to the fire boxes or tightening the ratchets on the barges. If he does not lose his pay immediately to some more skillful of his fellows on the boat, he preserves it only to see it vanish a few hours later in some shabby waterfront café.

The two chief forms of his gambling are dice and coon-can, the latter a simple card game related to the rummy of the whites. The dice playing is one of the most colorful spectacles on a steamboat, with its score of negroes gathered in a tense circle about the ivory cubes clicking steadily on the floor, while the blacks follow each throw with a rhythmic sigh like the hushed panting of the smokestacks. At the head of the circle sits a negro, with a great mound of silver before him and a loaded revolver in his hand. Sternly he presides over the game as banker and armed judge to arbitrate any disputes before they end in murder. Occasionally on a boat the gambling is organized, and the older roustabouts form a syndicate whose chief aim is to acquire all the money of the newcomers. The lot of the younger roustabout on such a vessel is burdened with melancholy.

The road of the roustabout gambler often leads to the jail door. Again and again, in the early morning, the kindly captain of a steamboat goes up the wharf to find one of his black laborers in the custody of the sheriff, and brings him back sad-eyed and murmuring apology. But all roustabouts are not gamblers. There are those who are deeply religious. There is scarcely a crew of roustabouts on the river which does not include a preacher; and I know one boat with a black crew totalling twelve of which three are practicing ministers of the Gospel. The roustabout parson's conversion may date from some tragedy; or it may be the result of natural piety finding expression after many years. The churches in which they officiate are pathetic: a bare little room with an old packing crate for a pulpit, and paper hanging in long mouldering strips from the broken walls. So poor are these churches that if it chances to be night, sometimes the preacher before commencing a sermon must take up a collection to buy kerosene for the oil lamp, so that the services may not be ended by darkness.

They are an amazing study in contrasts, these roustabout preachers, black giants who could fell an ox with a blow of their great fists, but who under the influence of their religion may become touched with a Christ-like spirituality.

The result of the roustabout's piety sometimes takes curious forms. I know one thoughtful steamboat preacher, who, despairing of ever obtaining a pulpit, was seriously considering a visit to a hoodoo doctor to secure a charm that would help him find a congregation. Another roustabout I knew, possessed of a beautiful voice, would never sing even a hymn, for fear of offending the Lord. And one rouster, believing he was in danger of dying, and uncertain of the creed which would bring him salvation, finally joined the Baptist, Methodist, and Catholic churches so that there could be no chance of a mistake.

I journeyed to a church not long ago numbering some roustabouts among its congregation, a bleak little building with the moonlight streaming through great holes in the roof. I mounted the platform and took a seat beside the preacher on the bench reserved for the visiting whites. An usher went about with a basket taking the collection. I made my contribution and sat watching.

The preacher, a gentle, white-bearded old man, counted up the result and shook his head in sadness. "All we got here is seventy-nine cents," he remarked wistfully. "Ain't there going to be nobody come up here and give us some more money?"

Not a soul moved in the sea of black figures before me.

The preacher counted the collection again as though he might change the result. He grew more dejected. "All we got here is seventy-nine cents," he repeated, his voice quavering till it seemed ready to break into a sob. "Ain't there going to be nobody come up here and give us some more money?"

There was again no stirring in the rows of figures sitting like black statues on the hard wooden benches.

The preacher breathed a sigh, and shook his head in resignation. "Well, if we ain't a-going to get it, I guess we ain't a-going to get it," he murmured. "I don't know what we'd a' done if it hadn't been for this precious white gentleman sitting up here on the bench giving us a quarter. We'd have fell mighty low."

The same mental quality that gives rise to so many preachers among the roustabouts makes them all deep philosophers. Though unable to read or write, they will sit for hours discussing some involved portion of the Bible with all the intensity of medieval theologians settling the problem of how many angels could dance on the head of a pin. I have sat with them far into the night explaining reincarnation, and discussing with them their preferences for an after life if the Hindu beliefs became actuality. Their answers were a poignant commentary on human aspirations. "I'd like to be a peacock," declared Two Bits, a little negro noted for his ugliness. "Everybody looks at a peacock. They has such a pretty tail."

While his companion, Sixty-One, a tall, sad-faced negro weary of battling a world of trial and pain, answered after long reflection that he would choose to be a milk cow. "Nobody ever hurts a milk cow," he said. "All they does is pet her, and give her all the hay she can eat, and blankets to keep her warm, and all the finest things there is anywheres. And when she gits sick, there's a doctor waiting right in the stable to give her some medicine. It'd sure be wonderful to be a milk cow."

The roustabout, like most negroes, is an accomplished singer. Whatever his task, rolling monstrous bales of cotton, or carrying heavy sacks of sugar or flour, he is always ready to break forth into some rhythmic chant that will help his liquid black arms and legs perform their strenuous labors.

A negro pulling with a dozen others at a rope to move a

barge will start to sing in a hushed voice laden with melancholy:

> "Vicksburg was a hilly town,
> Till the Yankees come and cut her down."

In a moment the whole toiling line is chanting in unison, their bodies swaying with a rhythm as sharp as the beating of a drum. The song grows louder, faster, until the long rope seems to vibrate with the rise and fall of their plaintive voices. Suddenly the deck boss grunts a command. The rope is dragged away. The song is ended. Only the first singer, reluctant to abandon the melody, still hums it faintly as he starts carrying the nail kegs with which the barge is loaded up the long hill.

But all the rousters' songs are not work songs. There are melodies they chant as they lie under the starry sky: songs about beautiful yellow-skinned girls with mouths full of bright golden teeth that shine like the setting sun. There are the blues, which old roustabouts have told me began when the "outlaw women" that followed the levee camps sat on the bank, and sang and played on mandolins, while the men coon-jined down the gangplank with their heavy loads. There are songs about steamboats and steamboat races:

> "The *Kate* and the *Nellie* had a race.
> *Kate* throwed water in *Nellie's* face."

There are songs of immediate events in their daily lives, composed by some unknown black poet as he sits at the end of a sultry summer day resting from his toil: the tragedy of a roustabout that killed the straight-haired girl who betrayed him, and now lies languishing in jail, awaiting the noose of the hangman; the eulogy of a rouster who bravely met death when he went out in a raging flood to rescue a drowning child. Whatever the song, it is generally in a low minor key, vibrant with sorrow, a reflection of the negro's tragic history.

The roustabouts live in a close-knit community. They lend each other needles to mend their torn clothing, and carefully trim each other's kinky hair; when one man catches a giant catfish it is a gay feast for all his fellows. Where there are no permanent quarters their beds may be an empty wheelbarrow or a strip of burlap stretched to form a crude hammock; in colder weather they may sleep in the warm, luxurious space over the boilers known as the St. Charles Hotel. Once chosen, the rouster acquires a rigid proprietary interest in the location; his fellows respect it as sacredly as though it were his cottage in some quiet river town. They make their own laws, with the deck boss and the mate as final judges and arbiters; when a thief, known as a cat, is discovered among them, punishment is swift and terrifying.

But if the roustabout has one outstanding quality, it is his superstition. As he is among the world's most inveterate gamblers, so is he high on the roll of its most superstitious. And with reason. Living on the water, his life constantly in peril from wreck, storm, or flood, there is little wonder that he comes to regard Old Al, the giant alligator who is god of the river, as an omnipotent, sometimes demoniac creature who must at all costs be placated. The Mississippi is a brooding stream, fringed with swamps and mystery; the world ashore is full of jails and sorrow. As a consequence the roustabout is always seeking some new way to outwit evil fortune, usually by means of a Tobey that will bring him luck at gambling. He is thus regal prey for every black charlatan who takes a shabby furnished room in the negro section and sets up his establishment as a hoodoo doctor. A hundred feet from the main street of one of the largest cities in the South is a drugstore where for a price of a few cents upward, every conceivable charm may be purchased, from Johnny Conquer Root, guaranteed to vanquish everyone you encounter, to scorpion dust that you can spill in your enemy's coffee, and see come to life as a scorpion once more, growing under his skin.

The hoodoo doctors of the Mississippi, like the voodoo practitioners of the West Indies, are direct descendants of the witch doctors I have watched in Africa, and their methods are varied as their own imaginations. Some equip their quarters with all the crawling creatures of the swamp: rattlesnakes, moccasins, lizards, and huge hairy spiders. Others, more sophisticated, rely on mechanical devices: a crystal, some whirling colored lights, or a few tricks of the amateur magician they have purchased in a magic store. As a spell they may give their client a hoodoo bag, made of red flannel wrapped around powdered rattlesnake and a piece of magnetized iron; the charm may be a scissors to cut the string with which the wife of a henpecked rouster is binding him to her. Whatever the method, it depends on fear; and the negro always emerges from the gloomy room convinced of the charm's efficacy.

I can testify to the reverence accorded these spell makers, for several times I have acted as a beneficent practitioner of the art of hoodoo. I was travelling on a steamboat one summer, when Turtle, a fat roustabout who knew my interest in such mysteries, plaintively requested that I give him a spell to make him stop gambling. He was tired of losing his money, he declared; at the end of each trip, he went ashore without a penny to show for his labor.

After some reflection I consented, and in the dark of the moon taught him this verse laden with magic:

"Gambler's money is not for me.
When I gamble my money rolls out to the sea.
Set my hand to shaking when I sit down by the cards."

When the verses had been mastered, I informed the earnest Turtle that in the future, whenever he was about to play cards, he would see his right hand shaking like a leaf in the wind. In addition, since a concrete object is of primary importance in the making of any spell, I gave him a capsule filled with a magical white powder which I had been employing as a miraculous preventative of malaria in the cypress swamps. Advising him to put the capsule inside the band of his hat, I announced that when the powder melted, the charm would be in effect.

I left the boat, and returning three months later, went below to seek out my patient. The other negroes were gathered in a tense circle, playing coon-can. But Turtle sat far away, watching with mournful eyes.

"How are you, Turtle?" I asked.

He shook his head in sorrow. "Captain, I played cards twice after you put that there on me. And the third time it come over me all of a sudden. And I can't play cards no more."

Now he always urges me to remove the spell. But so far I have not relented.

The hoodoo doctor generally contents himself with tricking his client out of all his earnings. At times, however, he extends his field of operations and engages in more criminal practices that may approach murder. There can be no question that on occasions negroes in the South are murdered by a hoodoo doctor at the request of some enemy burdened with a fat pocketbook. Whether the crime is accomplished through suggestion, by the wishing-to-death method, where the doomed man is modelled as a wax doll, and the hoodoo doctor thrusts a pin each day nearer and nearer the heart; or whether the killing is effected by arsenic or some other slow poison added to the victim's food, I cannot pretend to say. But I have spent too many days in regions of Africa where the witch doctors ply their trade, to declare flatly that it is all fraud, all charlatanry.

Hoodooing in America is by no means confined to the South. There are, perhaps, no Mississippi roustabouts in Harlem; but there is many a stuffy little room on Lenox Avenue where a charm may be purchased with all the ease of tropical New Orleans, only the price a trifle higher. And it has been but a few months since all work on the wharf of a Northern river town suddenly halted as the negroes were unloading one of the Greene Line boats that run between Cincinnati and Pittsburgh. A roustabout had found a needle and a fragment of red thread thrust into one of the sugar sacks piled near the vessel, an obvious sign that a hoodoo doctor was at work in the neighborhood; not a negro would raise a hand until Captain Tom Greene had hurried forward and thrown the needle into the river. One police chief that I know tries to protect the local negroes by forcing each arrested witch doctor to eat one of his own hoodoo bags.

The roustabout's superstitions do not extend, however, merely to the practitioners of hoodoo. They affect every part of his daily life. Not long ago Possum Joe, a rouster noted for his flippancy, was drowned, and the reason was obvious. Every moment Possum Joe kept throwing tobacco to Old Al

to make the river god smoke his pipe and create a fog, so that
the steamboat would tie up to the bank, and all work for the
day would be ended. Old Al grew irritated at last and ended
Possum Joe's impudence. If the roustabout's wife is suffering
from a tumor, a doctor may not be necessary: if the negro
can find a large snail and let it walk slowly across the swell-
ing, the trouble will vanish by morning. If a rooster is crow-
ing high up in a tree, he is not casually saluting the sun; he
is informing the captain and the crew that high water is on
its way, and they had better hasten to moor the boat safely in
a cove.

Ghosts are near the roustabout always. Scarcely a vessel on
the Mississippi fails to possess some spectral figure who returns from the other world to terrify the shivering black
laborers. There is a ghost on an Ohio steamboat with whom
I have long been acquainted. A roustabout was murdered on
the deck, and his body for several days was ferried back and
forth from the Kentucky to the Ohio shores, the Kentucky
authorities refusing to accept jurisdiction because the murder
was committed on an Ohio boat, the Ohioans refusing with
equal vigor because they insisted the crime was committed
on the Kentucky side of the river. Ever since, the spirit of
the murdered negro has been forlornly wandering up and
down the river, seeking a final resting place.

And little Piece O' Man constantly sees the ghost of his
dead comrade, Chattanooga. "That there Chattanooga was
the smokingest rouster I ever seen," he will tell you. "Used
to spend all his money gitting wonderful cigars. He kept 'em
in the icebox to have 'em tasting right, he said. Every night
after supper, he'd take one out and smoke it, and make big
smoke rings come up in front of him. And when he had three
of the rings going in a row, he'd take a match that was burn-

ing and throw it through 'em, all three of the rings at once. He seen it in a show, he said. One night he was wheeling coal off the fuel flat, and fell in the river, and was drowned. And I never expected to see Chattanooga no more. But sure enough, next night, the door of the icebox come open, and I seen him standing there, taking the cigars and feeling 'em to pick out the best one, like he always done. Then he set down and started blowing the smoke rings. He blowed the rings all right. But when he tried throwing the match, he couldn't get it through more than two. Every night he comes and tries to git the three. It makes him awful mad, and he sits there cussing, and burning his fingers. But he can't git the three no-ways."

There are ghosts that dwell on the land as well. A roustabout from the *Tennessee Belle,* when on a journey to Kansas City, met in a restaurant a beautiful negress, the loveliest girl he had ever seen in his many wanderings. They had supper together, then went off to a little café, and danced gaily until dawn, when she suddenly made her excuses and vanished. Six nights in succession she met him, then on the seventh failed to appear. A week passed and the roustabout grew frantic; for the first time in his life he had fallen desperately in love. She had written her name and address on a piece of paper, but in a careless moment he had mislaid it somewhere in his room. He began a feverish search for the precious fragment, found it toward midnight, and hiring a taxicab happily set out to visit her home. The cab drove for miles through the city and its dark outskirts, then halted at last at the address written on the paper. The roustabout disembarked. The car was standing at the gate of a cemetery. The girl had once been the negro belle of Kansas City and had died in a fever epidemic fifty years before.

The roustabout is superstitious, spendthrift, shiftless; he is pointing nowhere, and never arriving. In a highly efficient world there would perhaps be no place for him and his fellows, and he could only languish and die. Yet I hope he will long be spared. For as he goes his carefree way, rolling his cotton or his dice under the moonlit sky, he is one of the most colorful figures in the rich museum that is America. Perhaps in the future he will be threatened with extinction under the Juggernaut of some supermechanical monster whose only song is the horrible squeaking of machinery, and which can lift its cotton bales ten thousand at a time. But if he is thus menaced, there are many who will hope that Old Al, the river god, will arise in his wrath and annihilate the monstrous machine with his rushing waters, and leave behind only a trail of muddy steel and twisted wire. And over the watchers standing along the shore will steal a great contentment and peace, as from the distance there rises a chant, hushed, but joyous:

"Captain, Captain, is your money come?
I jest wants to know, 'cause I wants to borrow some."

III

SHANTYBOAT

THERE is a last frontier in America where men still live with their fishing lines and rifles in almost as primitive a fashion as the pioneers who set out for the West a hundred and fifty years ago. This frontier extends along the Mississippi River and its tributaries, from the hill-girded banks of the Ohio to the moss-hung bayous where the river meets the Gulf; the frontiersmen are the shanty-boaters who moor their craft between the cypresses, or in a forgotten cove along the willowed shores.

Often this frontier passes within a few hundred feet of some of the great inland cities of America; but the nation as a whole knows less of the shantymen who form such a picturesque segment of its population than it knows of the natives of Bali or Timbuctoo.

A shantyboater is perhaps America's oldest and closest approach to a gypsy, only instead of rolling along in a jolting wagon, he chooses the water as his broad highway. How many of these strange wanderers there are, no one knows. I have been far up the Big Sandy and the Cumberland, where the rivers wind through mountains rustling with forests of virgin pine. I have been down the bayous choked with water lilies and flaming with strange tropical flowers. I have been up the Kanawha, the Red, and the drowsy Ouachita, down the Atchafalaya, Grand River, and the storied Bayou Teche. I have travelled in steamboats, fishing boats, flat boats, and pirogues. And everywhere there were shantyboaters.

Once I estimated their number as thirty thousand. But this was a guess, based on my journeys among them. There has been no census of shantymen, for the census is the Government, and shantyboaters do not like the Government. That is the reason why they are shantyboaters. They are the original rebels, the perfection of rugged individualists. If a shanty-boater saw a census taker approaching, he would be certain the visitor was a revenuer come to look for a hidden still; or at the very least a truant officer seeking to drag his luckless children off to school, where they would be forced to sit at a desk all day, instead of being in a rowboat on the river watching the white cranes fly against the sky. Perhaps some day an enterprising sociologist preparing a thesis for a degree of Doctor of Philosophy will go out and count them. It would be a fascinating exploration. And when the count ended, he would be old and mellow and rich in the knowledge of mankind. For he would be compelled to catch them first.

He would meet some highly interesting people. For example, there is Catfish Johnny, a tall, rangy individual wearing a battered black sombrero, and always badly in need of a shave. When he works, which is not so often as to make life the burden it is for foolish people in cities, Catfish Johnny is a practitioner of that ancient craft of the river which may have come down from the Indians, the art of willow weaving. Out of the branches of the willows growing everywhere along the bank, he can fashion beautiful chairs which he will sell at prices ranging from twenty-five cents for the smaller pieces to a dollar for a vast arm chair that would support a giant. I happened to be visiting him one afternoon when he was hard at his labor, and had just sent out his son to bring in some boxes floating down the water. The son, a serious youth, with brilliant red hair and overalls that were mostly patches, returned soon after and set the boxes at the door.

Catfish Johnny studied them in sorrow. "These here's all Florida orange boxes," he lamented. "All the time you been a-bringing me them Florida orange boxes. Can't you get me no California orange boxes?"

The red-haired youth shook his head. "Ain't nothing anywheres but the Florida orange boxes. California orange boxes ain't come in yet."

Catfish Johnny's face grew tragic. "Doggone, I don't know what I'm going to do if I don't get some of them California orange boxes."

It seems he uses the wood for the bottoms of the willow chairs, and without intending any disrespect to the state of Florida, my shanty friends declare that the California orange boxes make much better seats.

It is easy for Catfish Johnny or any other expert to build a shantyboat. If he is patient, as good shantymen are, all the timbers and planks he needs will eventually come drifting down the muddy water. Or he can do some odd jobs at a lumber yard, and a good-natured foreman will overpay him in scrap lumber. To this he adds some discarded packing crates, a strip of tar paper obtained by more odd jobs in the hardware store, and a few window panes collected where a house is being dismantled; his materials are now all supplied.

With the help of his family or his neighbors, the new craft is quickly born. He adds a porch at the rear where he can sit and fish and chew tobacco; a tin chimney is poked through the flat roof; and the craft is completed. This is the true, the original shantyboat.

There are other, odder craft. There is that lowest form of shantyboat known as a "doghouse," a few pieces of rusty tin set up on a flatboat. Once I encountered a shantyboat whose walls appeared to be made of discarded automobile license plates. And up Black River, some years ago, I saw a shantyboat two stories high. But this was only a rarity, a freak, like the three-legged cow, or Joey, the Alligator Boy, being exhibited in a circus side-show.

Many shantyboats are paintless, with the boards that form them nakedly exposed to the winds and rains of the river. Others are elaborately decorated in styles to suit the individual proprietor. I have seen shantyboats painted in stripes of red and white so that they resembled great peppermint sticks soaking in the water; I have seen them painted in black and white squares, like huge checkerboards. Curiously I cannot remember ever having seen a shantyboat with a name painted over the door. They are anonymous.

For further decoration, often the good shanty wife sets flower boxes in her windows, and plants them with nasturtiums and four o'clocks, the gift of the wife of some friendly farmer; she may train vivid-hued morning glories to grow up a lattice, sheltering the porch from the view of passers-by. For more practical purposes, she may set out some beehives, so that the family will not want for sweets in winter; often she has a little raft moored alongside where a shabby rooster struts with his clucking harem about a wire enclosure. And should she chance to be a member of the shantyboat aristocracy, near the chickens there will waddle a pig.

The interior of a shantyboat is simple as the exterior. If it is a small craft, it contains a single room, with a sink, a table, a bed, a few boxes that answer for chairs, a battered stove— and always a dilapidated dog. Larger vessels may contain two rooms, even three.

Shanty dwellers become very ingenious in meeting the peculiar conditions of their lives. I know one old shanty wife who grew weary of seeing her rickety stove knocked down by the waves of every passing towboat. Lashing all her wooden furniture to the walls with ropes, she bound the stove with heavy wire, and from that time on was able to make her toilet or fry her bacon without the mirror or the stovepipe toppling on her head.

Decoration flourishes inside as well as out. Every wall is covered with pictures, for nowhere on earth is there a greater lover of art in all its diverse forms than the Mississippi shantyman. By the window will hang a gaudy print revealing the sinking of a great ship at sea, with hundreds of hands stretched out of the black water in desperate supplication; next it is a Sunday school print, portraying a scarlet-bearded Joshua stopping the movement of a purple sun. On the other side of the room is a calendar bearing the figure of a barefoot boy sitting sorrowfully beside a sick dog, with a painted legend overhead, announcing that for any emergency the best drugs may be purchased at the Excelsior Pharmacy; near by hangs a photograph of a white-bearded patriarch lying in his coffin.

Most shantyboaters are of English-Irish stock, and are closely related to the poorer natives of the Southern mountains. Often at New Orleans I have found a shantyman who has come from some upland county in my native Kentucky, and who sits beside his stove singing "Barbary Allen" in the high nasal fashion of the Cumberlands; while his wife embroiders a coverlet with the same "Rocky Road to California" pattern that I have seen so often in the foothills. Many are mountain people who succumbed to the lure of the cities, Louisville, Cincinnati, St. Louis, Memphis, and obtained work in the factories. But soon these transplanted frontiersmen rebelled against the thundering of machines and the punching of time clocks; finding some planks on a sand bar, they built little shantyboats, and drifted down the river to freedom.

For of all free lives in this machine-riddled world, there is none so free as the life of the shantyman. There is no burdensome rent to pay and no galling interest on a mortgage; there is no water or gas meter in your cellar ticking away your pennies with the finality of death. To secure water you need only dip a bucket over the side; to find fuel pick up some brush along the shore. When hunger assails you, bait a hook and catch a catfish; if it is land food that

you crave, this too is easily provided, for it is a stern and
unusual valley farmer who does not abide by the ancient
tradition that the last three rows of a riverside cornfield or
potato patch belong to the shantyman.

And where else could be found such a fascinating neighbor
as the Professor?

It was a warm, pleasant afternoon when I met the Professor, a kindly, white-bearded old man, living deep in
the cypresses. So hidden was his shanty by the trunks of the
twisting trees and the Spanish moss drooping from the
branches, only the little porch was visible; near it a great
water moccasin was crawling oilily. I had brought the Professor some milk chocolate, with which my pockets were always filled on these excursions, for dainties were scarce among
my friends; we had been sitting for a long time, nibbling,
and talking of the strange ways of the bayous and the river.
At last the sun began to set. Long white cranes sped past the
window and vanished in the shadowy trees. I took my hat
and rose to go.

The Professor grew troubled, wistful. "You haven't seen
her yet," he said.

"No, I haven't seen her," I answered hopefully, for I had
been told in advance about this mystery.

"Would you like to see her?" asked the Professor.

I nodded with enthusiasm.

A smile of deep satisfaction touched his wrinkled face. "I'll
show her to you," he declared.

We stepped onto another shanty moored alongside. Before
me there rose a gigantic wheel, like the flywheel of an engine, eleven feet high, and fitted everywhere with huge
weights and rusty chains.

The Professor's face glowed with pride. "She's a machine

for perpetual motion," he announced. "I'll show you how she works."

From a chest he extracted an iron handle, resembling the starting crank of an old-fashioned automobile, and inserted it in a slot at the center of the wheel. He tugged at the handle mightily. The great wheel rattled and creaked shrilly in protest, revolved a foot, and came to a dead stop.

The old man trembled with excitement. "She's a wonderful machine, ain't she?" he demanded, and awaited my verdict with anxiety.

"She's a beautiful machine," I answered truly.

His voice broke a little, so great was his joy. "I been a working on her twenty years. She's pretty near finished now. This year if the Lord just lets me keep on living, I'm a-going to get her done. And then I'm going to take her off to Washington and get her patented. I sure don't want nobody a-stealing that machine."

There are other racial stocks besides the English-Irish descendants that go to make up the shantyboat nation. In the southern reaches of the river, the predominant type changes sharply, and becomes the French-speaking fisherman, with his curious accent that legend says descends from the days when his ancestors paddled through the cypresses with the elusive Lafitte. And once, in Louisiana, I encountered on a shantyboat a family of European gypsies, who promptly, in the same fashion that their brothers elsewhere try to sell a broken-down horse or automobile, begged me to purchase some curious picture frames made of berries gathered in the swamps.

Like all other branches of human society, the characters of the individual shantymen vary widely. They divide roughly into two classes: the law-abiding, and those without

Shantyboat Preacher

the law. The separation is marked with a brilliant and indelible line, for the honest shantyman, rebel though he may be against the civilization of the world beyond, enacts his own code of law, and sees that it is rigidly enforced. Often I have watched a shantyman with a shifty, evil face and highly suspect character come to a colony of rivermen who dwell inside the law. For a few days, with philosophic calm, the presence and affronts of the newcomer are tolerated. Until some overt act is committed—a theft occurs, a blow is struck with a bottle. Instantly the council of the shantymen is called into session. That night, when the visitor is fast asleep, a chosen delegation of his neighbors goes out and cuts his mooring lines. And when he wakens, he has floated miles down the river, to trouble the rope cutters no more.

At times, when there is a shanty settlement that possesses some degree of permanence, the organization is considerably developed. My rusty friend, Catfish Johnny, the willow weaver, is the mayor of a little community of perhaps sixty people. Lazily he leans against a pillar of his porch and in his drawling voice makes Solomon-like decisions, settling a dispute between two neighbors as to the ownership of a choice cove on the river where the catfish bite the quickest. Or he sits gravely conferring with the other elders of the community, and after long deliberation decides what action is to be taken in the case of a diabolical river captain, who lets a huge chain hang over the side of his towboat, and tears to pieces any fish net that happens to be in the way. Another of my friends, nicknamed Big Sandy because his home lay up that mountain-born river, has learned how to spell, and does all the reading and writing for his fellows, collecting old newspapers in the town and telling his fascinated hearers what goes on in the world beyond the willows.

In such fixed settlements there is often the shantyboat preacher, sometimes self-ordained, sometimes one of the "Holiness Folks" or Holy Rollers. In his boat the shantymen gather for their services; though they possess no hymnbooks, a pious elder leads them in a hymn. Soon the tempo of the music quickens; hands begin to clap in explosive rhythm. And as the excitement increases, and the clapping of hands grows louder, faster, the worshippers leap wildly into the air, to show their devotion to the Lord. At such moments, the preacher begins the curious "talking in tongues," and though like his flock both reading and writing may be far beyond his powers, he and his parishioners firmly believe that he is speaking the Greek of St. Paul and the Hebrew of Moses, and sometimes even the Egyptian of Pharaoh. The preacher, because of his duties, has little time for his nets and lines, and is chiefly supported by the fish contributions of his congregation, which he trades at a neighboring plantation.

Bartering, such as the minister practices, is of primary importance in the life of the shantyman. The fishermen may exchange some of his shining buffalo for flour or part of a sugar-cured ham; he may trade catfish roe for a pretty dress grown too tight for its wearer, and bring it home to bedeck his sunbonneted wife. The income of the shanty family that has no definite occupation is incredibly low, perhaps eight dollars a year in cash. I have known cases where it was even less.

Shantymen, like all primitive people, may be difficult to meet, but once gained as friends, there is none more loyal. I shall not forget an experience up a winding stream toward the North. I had come to visit a shanty settlement that lay along the riverfront of one of the large cities in the valley, a shanty community with a bad name, inhabited by the more lawless of the river wanderers. The day before my arrival police had come on a sudden raid, and after a fierce battle half a dozen shantymen had been dragged off to jail. I noticed at once the shantyboaters' lack of cordiality, but knowing nothing of the events preceding, I could only wonder at the cause. Learning that most of the inhabitants were gathered in the shanty of an old woman called Aunt Sadie, I knocked softly on the door. I entered as a voice called out and saw ten or twelve gaunt shantymen, sitting on boxes, talking gravely, while the wrinkled Aunt Sadie stood making coffee over a rickety stove. The shantymen ceased their conversation to gaze at me with unconcealed hostility. Carefully I tried every means I knew to win their favor; with each effort their faces grew colder and colder. It was a very isolated settlement; I could have vanished from the world and only those on the shantyboat would have known the reason.

And then, as I watched Aunt Sadie toiling over the stove, inspiration struck me. It was obvious from her movements that the old woman was a careful housekeeper. The day was rainy and I had tracked mud everywhere with my shoes. Quietly I took a broom, and without a word, began to sweep the floor. Aunt Sadie looked in astonishment a moment.

Then her wrinkled face lighted.

"We thought you was a detective," she said. "But I know no detective ain't going to do no sweeping."

From that day on I was a friend of everyone in the colony.

The family relations of the shantymen vary as widely as the decorations on their walls. The men and women in the lawful group are devoted parents, and bring up their children in the best traditions of the shantyboater, teaching them to weave willow, to fish, and to avoid those criminal companions whose friendship would end in jail. Generally the sons and daughters marry other river girls and youths. But at times a river boy may wed a girl from the drowsy town or the green hills beyond the horizon; their fortune is awaited darkly, for tradition old as shantymen declares that never can a land girl make a true river wife. The men and women in the lawless group are not troubled with any permanent relationships, legal or otherwise.

An excellent place to encounter the shantyboater is the floating store or fish docks—to the river dweller what the crossroads grocery is to the rustic on the land. Here he can sit around the stove and chew his tobacco and ponder over the probable hour of the passing of the next towboat; here he can tell his tallest tales. These floating stores, now rare except in the southernmost tributaries, where fish is still an important article of commerce, are stocked with candy, razors, overalls, or anything which might strike the shantyman's restless fancy. The presence of a floating store indicates a high income from fishing; the shantyman here is the aristocrat of his kind, whose trade is to be sought and his favor cultivated.

To the shantyboater further toward the North, a good store is the Big Store. For the Big Store is the city dump from which wonderful treasures may be gathered: lamps whose shades are only a little cracked and which smoke only faintly; upholstered chairs embroidered with scenes of the Burning of Rome or the Pyramids of Egypt; or even a slightly damaged piano, to be saved for the long remembered evening when a grizzled shantyboat musician drifts past and pounds out on the yellowed keys: "Oh, I Don't Like a Steamboat Man."

But to the shantyboater on the main stream, the best store

is the river itself. For anything can drift down the water: a log; a tourist's rowboat broken loose from up stream with a basket of sandwiches and a wonderful bottle that keeps coffee hot for hours; or perhaps even a lady's hat and a coat with shiny pearl buttons. If it is high-water time, the prize may be a cotton bale or a roll-top desk full of cards covered with mysterious messages whose solutions will while away many a shanty night. And once, an old lady assured me, the prize was a bed complete with pillow and beautiful coverlets.

I was visiting at Catfish Johnny's one afternoon, discussing with him and his friends the weighty problem of whether the Mississippi was coming back to pick up the drift it had left two months before, when suddenly a black-bearded shanty-man standing in a corner ran to the window and looked out at the winding river. "Things is a-coming down!" he shouted.

The effect of the words on the others in the shanty was electric. Excitedly they rushed to take a place beside the observer, and pressed their faces against the glass.

"There comes a fine barrel!" cried Catfish Johnny.

"There's a wonderful table!" called his wife, a cheerful, blue-aproned little woman, who had darted in from the bed-room.

"And look at that there box!" shouted a gaunt figure in a pair of faded overalls. "Can't ever tell what you're going to get in a box thataway!"

They scurried out the door. Leaping into their rowboats, and seizing their oars, in an instant they were darting over the yellow water, in feverish pursuit of the treasures bobbing on the waves.

There are numerous industries for the shanty dweller. Besides the willow weaving, which Catfish Johnny practices, on the lower river and the bayous there is moss collecting; the

shantyman and his family pull down the Spanish moss drooping in rich pendants from the trees and sell it to the moss-
buying boat, to be made into mattresses. There is musseling—
catching the mussels and selling the shells to a button factory,
an occupation filled with delightful uncertainty, for now and
then within a shell there lies a mussel pearl. I have heard of
Mississippi pearls worth as much as three thousand dollars.
If the shantyman finds such a rarity, the effect is as if some
hungry wanderer on the Bowery by a miracle discovers himself to be the possessor of a winning sweepstakes ticket. More
than one shanty life has been revolutionized by such a discovery. But the change is only temporary. Soon the money is
gone, and the penniless prodigal is back on the river, searching for another pearl. Usually the prize is worth only a few
dollars.

But the main shantyboat industry is fishing, fishing for the
succulent cat and the shining buffalo. The quantities of Mississippi fish caught and sent to the East are astonishing in
their vastness. The glistening buffalo leaves its home in the
muddy water to be sold in the delicatessen stores of New
York's East Side as Russian sturgeon; the highly prized roe
of the yellow catfish may appear on Delancey or Rivington
Street as Russian caviar.

Fishing here approaches the proportions of a real commerce; when times are good, the shanty fisherman often
rises completely out of the category of his penniless brother
of the more northern waters. The catch is bought by the fish
docks or the larger packing houses, generally through the me-
dium of a fishing-boat captain who makes trips twice weekly
down the river and its tributaries. They are loyal, these
shantymen, and I have seen them let their fish rot in the
water rather than sell to a rival operator when their own cap-

tain's boat was delayed. The fishboats, because of the nature of their cargo, try to run with exacting regularity. So successful are they in keeping their schedules, there is a legend that when Captain Eli's fishboat was unable to start out on its usual Wednesday, but arrived on Thursday instead, most of the shanty people who were his clients, swore that the day *was* Wednesday. And it took a pronouncement from Captain Eli himself to set the calendar right again.

When the shantyman is far out in the cypress wilderness, the fishing-boat captain is his sole contact with civilization, being at once his doctor, his provider of entertainment, and even a matrimonial bureau. I know one captain who regularly brought up brides for lonely fishermen, married the bashful couples himself, and became furious when the romances did not last and he would be compelled to bring the young women back to town again.

The methods of obtaining a catch are unique, the oddest being the practice known to the initiate as "jugging fish." A vinegar jug may be useful to a shantyman as a musical instrument through which he blows strange melodies, but it has a practical value as well. The fisherman fits corks into half a dozen jugs to make them waterproof, ties on a fishing hook to each stony container, then links the jugs loosely with a line. A moment later, he sets them in the river, and letting them drift down the current, climbs into his boat and rows slowly behind. Suddenly a jug begins to dance excitedly. The fisherman rows toward it swiftly; for he knows that he has a catch. A later improvement in jug-fishing technique is to substitute a tomato can with a nail hung inside on a string, so that instead of merely bobbing up and down when there is a catfish or buffalo beneath, it rings out the cheerful tidings.

The bait is curious. To most small boys fishing is as ines-
capably connected with worms as lightning with thunder.
But this is not the case with the shantyboat fisherman. I
have never recovered from my initial shock of seeing these
river wanderers bait all their lines with bread. Actually, the
bait is a "dough ball," made of corn meal and flour to which
is added a little garlic.

It is a lazy life, the life of the shantyboat fisherman. There
is much time to talk. And there are few who are better con-
versationalists, with their mellow philosophy and vast store
of information, so much of it inaccurate. I know of nothing
more delightful than to sit in a flatboat while Catfish Johnny
runs his lines, and listen to him tell of the lore of the river:
how if you take a fish out of the Red River or Black River
and drop it in Mississippi water it will die as quickly as
though you had pierced it with a bullet; how fish will spoil
quicker in the moonlight than under the sun. He will tell
you how it is useless to fish after a night of bright moonlight,
because fish will gorge themselves feeding in the light of the
moon, and so the next day will bite at nothing; or how a
fish cannot be kept with its head down stream or it will
drown like a human. He will explain how if you wish to
catch an alligator, you must put a piece of garlic on a stick,
and when you poke this into the alligator's hole, the smell
will drive him out in panic; he will describe how the fish
travel on great highways through the water, just as if they
were on roads marked out by Government men.

For every catfish, there is a character, picturesque, fascinating. There is Whistling Tom, who beats his nets furiously
with a switch when they do not yield a good catch and pets
them like children when the results are favorable. There is
Black-Tie Jack, who, legend says, is an unfrocked preacher,

and Blind Frank, who will not leave the river, though he cannot see a candle before his eyes. There is John, the Atheist, who is always cursing God and shouting: "If God'd come down now I'd burn him in a gallon of gasoline," and who has been punished by seeing all his children born blind.

Vast swamps fringe the river in its lower reaches, where the shantymen wander aimlessly. The reputation of certain of these areas is dark and sinister, legend declaring that the twisting cypresses shelter murderers with rewards on their heads sufficient to buy all the towering buildings on Canal Street in New Orleans. For a shantyboat in the swamps is a perfect refuge. A sheriff entering the region is in the same perilous situation as a revenue officer making a raid in the Southern mountains; everywhere shantymen watch behind trees and windows to report the slightest movement of this invading enemy.

It was in one of these sections of evil reputation that I chanced to make an odd discovery. I had been traveling for four days in a small boat through a wilderness tangled with vines and poisonous flowers like the jungles of the Amazon

or the Orinoco, when I suddenly came upon a colony of
shanty fishermen. All were English, bearing usual English
names, like Bates, Black, and the omnipresent Jones. They
were proud of their English ancestors, these shantymen. They
boasted that they could not speak French, and would not
speak it if they could, because they scorned the French
tongue and their French neighbors. But for many generations they had been so surrounded by French-speaking people, they could only speak English with a French accent, so
thick and so curious it was only with difficulty I understood
a word.

As the swamps grow more dismal, the mosquitoes rise up
like poisonous vapors, and the superstitions increase. And
who is to say which superstition is based on fact and which
is wholly fancy? If a man is cut badly with a fish knife, let
him ask someone to row swiftly to Aunt Tate's shantyboat.
Or if Aunt Tate's dwelling is distant, let him find a messenger to go in the fishing boat and tell her the news. For if
the messenger arrives in time, Aunt Tate can pronounce a
magic spell out of the Bible and stop the bleeding instantly,
if the patient is not more than ten miles away. If his wife
has the earache let Aunt Tate blow into it, and thus extin-
guish the fire; or let him take two drops of blood from the
beetle known as the Betsy Bug, and allow these to trickle
into the ear cavity. If his baby is ill with that peculiar blis-
tered throat condition known as thrash, let the mother take
the shoe of a man who has never seen his father, fill it with
water before going to bed, then give the water to the child
as a gargle in the morning. Doctors have informed me this
favorite remedy may have some basis in science. The shoe
contains compounds of tannic acid, a drug common in the
treatment of certain throat maladies.

It is foolish for a shantyman to allow his dog to sleep on a pile of green Spanish moss, as the dog will surely sicken and die. It is equally unwise to mock a screech owl crying weirdly outside the door; the first time the shantyman is absent for a few hours, the bird will scratch hot ashes from the stove onto the floor, and the shanty will burn to the water's edge.

Once, deep in the swamps, I took advantage of the superstitious nature of the shantymen. A hurricane had swept the Gulf, and some sea gulls had blown far inland with the wind. The shantyboaters of the remote region I was visiting had never before seen these strange silvery creatures, and hurried to get rifles to shoot them for their suppers. I dreaded seeing the beautiful birds that soared so gracefully over the trees become the targets of such expert marksmen. But to have told my hosts not to shoot would have been far from tactful. So instead I began relating the story of Coleridge's Ancient Mariner, carefully changing the albatross whose slaying brought the Mariner such evil fortune to a sea gull. Not a shot was fired.

The shantyman's rifle is always ready at hand for other game than sea gulls, for in the Southern waters, hunting and trapping become one of his important occupations. Muskrat, coon, possum, and wildcat are his quarry, and in the wilder regions nearer the Gulf, he finds even an occasional panther.

As Catfish Johnny is the peer of shanty fishermen, so is Corporal Jeff the king of shanty hunters. Lanky, gaunt, like most of his fellows, possessing a silvery crescent moustache that he trims with exacting care, he stalks along the river accompanied by his two dogs whose ancestry is vague as the fogs of the gloomy swamps they roam. But though their lineage is not to be proudly proclaimed, their talents are prodigious. I have tracked through the steamy woods beside Corporal Jeff, and with my own eyes I have seen these dogs climb trees. There have been witnesses on other occasions to this same miracle. Truth must admit the trees had twisted, gnarled trunks that here and there gave a foothold, and were not poplars soaring straight into the sky. Nevertheless they were trees, with all a tree's difficulties. I have seen these dogs go swiftly up a trunk in pursuit of a hiding possum. I have also seen them coming down. And their usually amiable, flea-bitten faces at such times were not happy.

Corporal Jeff, as he sits chewing his tobacco, and curing a muskrat skin, can tell you much that is fascinating, even though, like Catfish Johnny's information, it may not always be too factual. He will explain, when you see a raccoon with a ragged tail, how this furry adventurer has been fishing for crabs. If you follow on one of the animal's excursions, you will see him halt at the river bank and move his tail slowly back and forth in the water until the great claw of a crab reaches out and seizes it in a fierce grip. Before the crab can let go again, the coon whisks the tail from the water, and the luckless crab drops like a stone to the bank. Corporal Jeff can tell of the gigantic loggerhead turtle, monarch of the swamps and the alligator's deadly enemy; he can describe the loggerhead's favorite method of fighting this huge lizard by snapping off a leg with a single fierce bite. And he can tell you of snakes.

Corporal Jeff knows the whip snake, that sucks the milk from a straying cow, and then viciously beats the unfortunate animal so that it will go out and graze again, to make more milk to drink. He knows the venomous joint snake, that breaks into a dozen little snakes, all more poisonous than the first, which close about the luckless victim in an ever tightening circle. And Corporal Jeff knows that deadliest of all serpents, the stinging snake, who possesses in his tail the peculiar attachment that gives him his name, a long stinger that goes up and down like the needle of a sewing machine, and which is loaded with venom so dreadful a cobra becomes as a gentle child by comparison. For if in its fury the great serpent happens to sting a tree, even a veteran oak or cottonwood that has withstood years of tempest and flood, that tree dies within three days.

The relations of the shantyboatmen with the steamboaters depend upon the individual. With some there has been no pause in the age-old feud, that breaks out anew whenever the paddle wheel of a steamboat causes a shantyboat to rock crazily. I knew a pilot who came from a river where the shantymen had been his friends, to a bayou where they were bitterly hostile, because of the sins of a previous captain who had delighted in annoying the proprietors of the little craft moored along the bank. I chanced to be with him on his first trip, and as the vessel passed a gray-painted shantyboat, he saw a pretty girl standing near the porch, hanging out the washing. The pilot blew the whistle gaily in salute. To his astonishment, instead of waving as had been the fashion of the girls on the river from which he had just departed, she stared at him coldly, and in a moment her father appeared holding a rifle. The pilot blew the whistle no more.

It is much better for both when they are friendly. A steamboat captain may be particularly helpful in the grave problem of shantyboat transportation. A shantyboat needs no assistance moving down the stream, but coming up it fails woefully, for there is no motive power. To take the place of an engine there is cordelling, that now rare practice of tying a rope to a tree a hundred feet up the shore, and winding the shanty to it with a windlass. But this method is laborious, and progress infinitesimal. A few of the richer shantymen own second-hand motors which they purchased for a few dollars and restored to asthmatic life. But such aristocrats are unusual; the others must wait patiently for the fish buyer's craft or a passing steamboat whose captain will give them a tow. The shantyman can be of equal aid to the steamboater. He can supply fresh catfish and turtles for the cook's galley; at times he can give a quiet warning that will prevent the looting of a wharf boat by marauders drifting down the river.

There is a childish, a pathetic simplicity about the shantyman's pleasures and desires. A toy dog which runs in a circle chasing its tail, perhaps found in a box drifted down on a flood; a bottle filled with colored water; a paper weight of different colored stones glued under glass and labelled "Souvenir of Denver, Colorado"—such treasures are enough to excite them to transports of delight. And their curiosity about the outside world which most of them know they will never see is equally touching. Once I visited a little woman with clear blue eyes and finely chiseled face, living all alone in a trim little shanty far up the Red River. Unable to read or write, she sat alert in her chair all during my stay, plying me with questions, and when I started to take my leave, said to me wistfully: "Would you mind a-writing down on a piece of paper the names of all the places you been and a-giving it to me? I'd sure be mighty proud of having a wonderful paper like that."

This pathetic childishness is magnified by the contrasting difficulties of their lives and their constant nearness to calamity and death. A huge alligator gar, with a head like a nightmare, rips their nets to pieces and in a moment destroys the labor of weeks; the oil company builds a dock at Baton

Rouge, and the oil leaking into the water drives the fish far away. A hurricane sweeps in from the Gulf or a tornado roars out of the West; the shanty is wrecked, and half the family drowned. A gigantic tree falls upon the frail dwelling, crushing it to kindling, or a steamboat destroys it in a fog; the shantyman builds a new craft and starts his life all over. And no matter whence the blow comes, his spirit is always the same, a combination of stoicism and cheerfulness that enables him to meet any disaster. As Catfish Johnny met his tragedy.

I visited Catfish Johnny often, bringing a cake for him and his gay little wife. They were an unusually fortunate shantyboat family, with nothing to disturb their tranquillity; the money Catfish Johnny earned by his chair-making provided them with luxuries denied most of their neighbors. Then one day a city man came to visit, who declared he was weary of the drab existence of the town and wished to become part of the life of the river. He had a brand new automobile, he declared. Would Catfish Johnny care to trade his shantyboat for the car?

Catfish Johnny and his wife were dazed by the offer. No shantyman they ever dreamed of had possessed an automobile. For years they had talked of what it would be like to roam the unknown territories beyond the riverbank. Now here was opportunity, as though sent by Heaven. For several days they hesitated, then after long councils with their shanty neighbors, at last succumbed to the visitor's persuasions. The trade was quickly made. Catfish Johnny and his wife and son began moving all their possessions out to the automobile. Carefully they piled their mattresses on the top; lovingly they tied the boxes of dishes and the pictures and the fishing lines along the back and the running boards. Coaxing their wondering dogs inside, they set out to explore the universe.

For a few days all went rosily. I saw them going down the main street of the little town near by, with Catfish Johnny at the wheel learning to drive. His unshaven face and that of his wife were ecstatic; their dogs were barking excited salutes to every passer-by. They recognized me and waved happily.

A month later I was down at the riverbank, and I saw Catfish Johnny cutting willows.

"How's the car?" I inquired solicitously.

He brushed the perspiration from his forehead and shook his head a little sadly. "Things ain't a-been so good," he said. "Looks like we kind of lost her. We was getting along fine in her for about a week and we was a-figuring some fine places to go, New Orleans, and maybe some of them places way out there in Texas, when a policeman come up to me all of a sudden and hollered: 'Where'd you get that automobile?' I told him I done traded it for my shanty. 'It's a stolen car,' he said. 'Git out before I put you and your old woman and your dog in jail and hang you.' And so I got out, like he said. I went down to the river to try to find my shanty. The fellow wasn't no riverman and she'd got smashed to pieces. Me and the old woman's got a piece of tin now we kind of got on the bank for a house. She's a-getting it fixed up mighty pretty inside. I found her a roll of wallpaper they was throwing away in a store up in town. It's sure a wonderful paper. Got cows a-standing under trees all over it. The old woman'd mighty like it if you'd come down and eat some supper. I done caught a mighty fine catfish."

With all its perils and tragedies—the flood waters that carry everything before them and the caving banks that sweep down like a mountain avalanche—it is a beautiful life, the life of the shantyboater, for any wandering spirit weary of a strife-torn world. For where else can be found an existence as untrammeled? There is always something coming down the river. And there is always a white crane flying against the sunset. And there is always a steamboat blowing for a landing, and the whistle makes as sweet music as has been heard this side of the sky. Or if it is music nearer at hand for which the soul hungers, Catfish Johnny or Corporal Jeff or Big Sandy can always pick up a harmonica or a guitar or a vinegar jug, and as the drowsy birds chirp faintly in hushed accompaniment, go drifting down the water—to peace.

Government Fleet

IV

THE ENGINEERS

WHEN the casual American sitting at a hamburger stand in Wichita or before the marble tables of a restaurant in San Francisco's Chinatown chances to think of the United States Army, he envisions the long rows of soldiers he has seen passing in review on some wind-swept parade ground; he remembers all the wars through which he has lived or read of in his histories. He thinks of Zachary Taylor on his troubled way through Mexico and Custer before the destroying Indians; he thinks of the rout at Bull Run, and the charge at San Juan Hill, and the fierce fighting at Château Thierry along the quiet Marne.

Yet versed as he may be in the country's military history, unless he is a rare American he has no slightest inkling that the army is today engaged in a war with a battle front two thousand miles long, reaching from the bustling Twin Cities of Minnesota to the mosquito-fringed shores of the Gulf of Mexico. It is a war which curiously causes its armies to leave the land that is always the domain of the soldier, and compels them to take to boats and go out as sailors over the water. The sea they sail is the yellow Mississippi; the mariners are the army engineers who patrol the great stream, waging a never-ending war with Old Al, the River King.

It is a strange, peace-time war, with the blowing up of an abandoned levee or the dynamiting of a menacing snag its substitutes for exploding shells. But it is a relentless war; a war of merciless Nature pitted against man. It is a war of two major battles, the battle of drought and the battle of flood, the struggle in periods of low water being to keep the channel open so that the boats may travel, the combat in floodtime being to confine the raging waters to their banks so that they will not sweep the Valley to destruction.

It is a war of many and complex phases, calling for all the warrior's science and his guile. For King Al, the giant alligator who is monarch of the river, is an ancient and a wily sovereign. In his long life he has employed a thousand channels from which he wanders back and forth, carelessly and wilfully; he may choose or abandon any of the thousand between the rising and the setting of the sun. It is the task of the engineers to keep him confined in one.

The labor is full of difficulty and peril. From the sources of the tributaries high in the Alleghenies and the Rockies, to the drowsy fishing boats at the mouth the engineers roam, measuring, studying, here hurrying the water's flow with a deep cut along a sandbar, there checking it with a wooden dike or a dam. One day their neighbor is a lonely mountaineer tending his corn patch on a piney slope, the next it is a huge alligator sunning himself on a rotting log in a gloomy cypress swamp. They are the friends of the hermits and the outcasts of the world who have fled for refuge to the dark woods. They ask nothing, hear nothing, see nothing. For their work and their lives are at the mercy of these dwellers of the wilderness, and a dead engineer builds no levees. I have heard rumors in my travels of engineers carrying piles of sugar belonging to a friendly moonshiner onto one of their barges to keep this essential of the still from being destroyed in a rain. I have heard of an engineer who helped the wife of an ill moonshiner complete the husband's monthly run of whisky and prepare it for the customers.

So proverbial are the engineers' wanderings there is a legend that a traveler one day after weeks of exploration arrived at a vast wilderness of virgin pine and cypress which he was certain had never before been seen by the eyes of a white man. Exulting in his discovery, and reflecting on the honors and rewards that would come to him as the finder of this magnificent forest, he pitched his tent, and was frying some bacon, when the loud squawking of a bird attracted his attention. Looking up he saw a tattered parrot, obviously a veteran resident of the region, sitting on a branch of an old pine tree which served as his home. The parrot was shouting some curious words the traveler could not understand. He walked closer. The parrot, unafraid, did not move and squawked louder.

"Get out of the way, damn you!" it shouted. "Can't you see I'm running a transit line?"

The face of the traveler grew pale. His joy of discovery

faded. The U. S. Engineers had been there long before.

The most mobile of the vessels the engineers employ are the snub-nosed survey boats. Manned by civilian crews of typical Mississippi steamboatmen like most of this odd navy, the little vessels go out twice each week to sound the yellow water and set buoys to mark the channel so that the great towboats with their cargoes worth millions may pass safely through. All day the little vessels steam along the river, halting, reconnoitering; all day a rustic white youth stands at the bow casting the lead, and announcing the markings on his line in a high rhythmic call that varies between a chant and a wail.

The captain begins to steer the vessel back and forth in the process known as "feeling a reef."

The calls of the youth come faster, with their phrases different than the markings used on the steamboats. "Fourteen a-feet!" he wails. "Thirteen a-feet! O twelve a-feet!"

On the deck above him stands another rustic with a row of red and black buoys shaped like torpedoes poised at the vessel's edge.

"Watch the red buoy!" calls the captain, steering the boat toward a white sandbar that stretches off into the distance.

"O ten a-feet!" chants the youthful leadsman.

"Let her go!" shouts the captain.

The red buoy, like a giant flying fish, leaps out from the boat and cascades into the water. Another and another follow. Soon behind the vessel there is a bobbing red trail, like some scarlet sea monster come up to investigate this new world of the river; after a time black buoys flash one by one over the side, and a speckled black streak follows the boat, as though it were the red monster's mate.

The work of the survey boats is ceaseless as the rising and setting of the sun over the gnarled cypresses. For the reefs shift with a suddenness that astonishes even the veteran observer of the river. A buoy placed over a shoal three feet in depth on Tuesday, may be in water thirty feet when the boat steams past on Friday; within two weeks a reef may shift a quarter of a mile. Strange, unexplainable things occur in the river bottom. On one occasion, in the dead of night, when the boat was anchored near a grove of cottonwoods, the sleeping crew was suddenly awakened by a terrific rocking, with waves breaking over the pilot house so enormous that only the captain's expertness saved the vessel from capsizing. Five minutes afterward the river was smooth as a mirror. There had been no clouds, no wind; the Gulf, whose tides might cause such a phenomenon, was a thousand miles away. The captain instantly ordered soundings. The boat had been pulled up to the shore at the edge of a sandbar with only three feet of water beneath its tiny propeller; when the leadsman threw his line there was now a hole fifty feet deep and half a mile long. The entire sandbar had either made a sudden shift and moved in a huge earthen mass further down the water, or it had dropped into some quicksand pocket far below the muddy bottom in a sort of river quake.

The crews of the survey boats are always in the midst of exciting adventures. The deck hands must be as expert lassoers as the cowboys on the red-tinted plains of New Mexico. When a reef shifts, the channel markers become useless; it is the deck hand's task, while the boat steams near, to cast his lassoo over the buoy and bring it aboard as though it were a steer he was roping in a roundup. When buoys mysteriously disappear, they must seek out the reason. They may find the offender is some shantyboat newcomer, who, unfamiliar with the code of the river, has cut up a buoy that he might attach its minute rudder to his own gas boat; they must track him down and see that the crime is committed no more. One day they will be rushing a dying fisherman to the hospital; the next they will be speeding into some malarial swamp to rescue an adventurous child run off to hunt with a bow and arrow in the moss-hung haunts of the moccasins.

Their adventures may be droll as well, inspired by the robust sense of humor which is one of the riverman's chief possessions. "We had a funny time down by Scrubgrass Bend on a survey boat," my lean, rusty friend, Corn Beef Harry, a veteran deck hand of the engineer boats told me, as he cast a line in the forlorn hope of finding a catfish for his supper.

"There was a farmer down there had a smart-aleck calf was always getting into trouble, bullying the other calfs, and fighting his mother. And one day we was tied up by the bank and he come nosing around for something to eat, and before we could stop him, he'd broke up half the dishes in the kitchen. Next time we landed he come down again, looking for more devilment, so we figured we'd fix him. We tied him up so he couldn't kick, and then we painted big red and white stripes all over him till he looked like a zebra that was eating too much peppermint candy. Then we turned him loose on the bank. He seen his mother, and went over kind of whimpering to tell her his troubles. But she just give one look, and then went flying across the field like she'd chewed a wasp's nest instead of her cud, and letting out bellows you could hear in New Orleans. And all the other calfs give one look, and they started running and yelling like the cow. Then a big bull come up to see what was going wrong, and he stood there watching the painted calf, and grumbling like thunder. And all of a sudden he reared up and come charging like a lion across the grass. I figured the cow had run pretty fast, but she was like a snail on crutches to the way that calf run to the woods, with the bull a-roaring after him. He didn't come back for a couple of weeks, when the paint was all wore off him. And he was sure a changed calf. All his smart-aleckness was gone. He didn't do no more fighting, or nosing around, or nothing. All day he just tended to his own business and did everything his mother and the big bull said. There's a couple of smart-aleck steamboat captains on the river I wish I could paint with stripes like that. Me and some of the boys 'd buy the finest paint there is."

In each of the distant engineer offices there is a large map where every slightest variation of the river is carefully noted, as though it was the fever chart of a patient in a hospital. The charts at length indicate that the condition of the patient is perilous; the channel is filling. Instantly a dredge boat is dispatched to dig it free. For a sandbar developing under the yellow water would mean the halting of the vessels with their rich cargoes and at times even their destruction.

It is a huge, awkward creature, the dredge boat, like an elephant with an enormous trunk that stretches an eighth of a mile across the river, a huge pipe line with which it sucks up the gluey mud of the river bottom. Day and night it labors, pumping, grumbling, moving forward foot by foot, ceasing only for a few moments to clean away the timber clogging its vast metal mouth, or when it must swing its long trunk aside to let some impatient steamboat pass.

Like their fellows of the survey boats, the crews of the dredges are ever in the midst of some new excitement. One day the pumps will bring up a few mouldering doubloons, from the time when the conquering Spaniards roamed the countryside; the next they will unearth some buffalo horns, relics of the days when the buffalo were so thick steamboats were forced to halt for hours while the animals swam past on one of their great migrations. Now and then they will find a rusty cannon ball fired in the War between the States; occasionally they will make a grimmer discovery, the skeleton of some unfortunate traveler killed by river pirates as he came floating down on a raft from the North.

"Always something doing on a dredge boat," drawled Corn Beef Harry as he cast his line again. "But best of all is goose hunting. You're in one place a long time and that way you get to know the woods and things. First you cut yourself a decoy goose out of a flat piece of tin. And then you dig a pit out on a sandbar and get down inside. Pretty soon a lady goose comes along, that's looking for a husband maybe, and she sees the tin goose and he looks pretty good. So she starts walking up and down in front of him, fluffing up all her feathers mighty fancy. But he don't pay no attention. Then she starts flying to show him how pretty she is in the air, and the minute she gets over him, she can't see him no more, 'cause he's just a flat piece of tin, and don't show edgewise. She gets kind of worried, and lights to the ground again. Sure enough, there he is, not paying any kind of attention to her. She gets mad now, 'cause she figures he's just trying to make a fool of her. And when she flies up a couple of more times and the same thing happens, she goes kind of crazy, and comes over close to scream out what a lady thinks of him, like your wife when you get back from a trip and you're short four cents in your pay. When a woman goose is yelling that-a-way, you don't need a gun. All you got to do is put out your bare hand. Looks like all women's alike.

They're always a-hollering, but a riverman can fool 'em every time."

But of all the engineer boats, perhaps the most adventurous are the snag boats, those squat, curious-prowed vessels that go out to clear the channels of the great trees lodged in the bottom, so that their jagged arms may not pierce the hulls of the vessels blundering against them in the darkness. For six or eight months they may be away from their home ports, voyaging up some narrow tributary in a desolate wilderness. Once I visited a snag boat whose crew had been absent from their homes for over a year, and still had no idea of when they would be returning. Their lives are unpredictable. Every storm that snaps a tree, every flood that washes down the loose timber on the banks creates new problems. And time after time, just after a section of the river has been cleared of its obstructions so that the course is straight as the cinder path for some fleet Olympic runners, there will come a new wind or downpour, and the task must be started all over again.

It is dangerous work, this snagging. The captain sits in the pilot house watching the river alertly. Suddenly he sights a half-submerged log anchored squarely in the channel. Expertly he maneuvers the boat till the U-shaped prow is directly over the obstruction; a huge pair of tongs hanging from a frame, as though for a giant iceman, is lowered until it hooks into the sunken wood. An engine coiling a metal cable starts to turn noisily; the tongs bite deeper and deeper, and tug fiercely at their prey. Suddenly, with an explosive splashing, the log jerks free. In a moment, like some captured animal, it lies prostrate on the deck. Swiftly the deck hands attack it with huge saws; soon nothing remains except some blackened sections of timber floating like slices of some odd buoyant sausage down the water.

The snag boats, like the dredges, often find unusual prizes. Sometimes a hollow log will be filled with fish; I know one captain who in this manner caught two immense catfish weighing more than sixty-five pounds. Constantly they bring up mussels which the crew eagerly search for pearls; occasionally the unexpected catch is a huge alligator, who sends the boat into a momentary fever before it is driven back to its watery home. Since the vessel is generally far from civilization, game of all kinds is common. And the captain of one snag boat, as a Government official, was called upon to help hunt down a huge monster whose like had never been seen in the countryside, an enormous water creature eighty or a hundred feet long, so powerful rumor declared it had pulled the ferryboat at a near-by settlement ninety miles without stopping for breath.

"But funniest thing I ever knowed about was a time on one of them wild little rivers goes way up in the mountains," Ratty Joe, the dwarfish deck hand and handyman on a snag boat told me as he sharpened a saw for the vessel's carpenter. "Captain and everybody went off to a farmhouse where they was having a big dance or something. Wasn't nobody on the boat but me and the assistant engineer that was just a kid. I was trying to get some sleep. All of a sudden I wake up and hear something walking up and down outside my cabin, a-blowing like a railroad locomotive. I look out, and there's the biggest panther I ever seen. He must have been terrible hungry or something, 'cause pretty soon he smelled me, and he started howling and tearing down the door. I didn't have a gun, so I knew I'd have to do something mighty quick. I yell down to the kid in the engine room, and he answers, and then I open the back door of my cabin, and run fast as I can to the end of the boat and climb out on the paddle wheel. In a minute the panther comes after me. But I knew that wheel better than him, 'cause it was breaking down all the time, and we was always having to fix her. When the panther got to the wheel, he kind of slowed up, 'cause he didn't like the looks of it, and then he climbed on too. And quick as a monkey, I swings down to the deck below.

" 'Give it to her,' I yells to the kid in the engine room.

"The big cat started coming down, stepping mighty careful. And in a minute he'd a-had me, when the engine gives a hiss and the wheel starts turning. The panther looked mighty surprised, but he must have been part squirrel or something, 'cause when the wheel started going faster and faster he kept a-running with it, just like a horse in them what they calls treadmills I seen once in a big show was at St. Louis. But pretty soon the wheel got to turning like it was crazy, and even the panther couldn't keep up with it no more, and all of a sudden he give an awful yell, and went flying into the river. I couldn't even see him when he come out on shore, he was going so fast. And I don't like to do no exaggerating, but next day there was a big open space in the woods where he run through, just like there'd been a tornado. People over at Parmelee, that was fifty miles away, said they heard a terrible lot of noise that night and got up and seen the biggest shooting star was ever in the county whizzing through the sky. But way I figure, what they seen was the panther."

The work on land of the engineers is as colorful as their work on the water. A spectacular labor is the making of a gigantic mat, either of concrete blocks or willow trees, to reinforce the banks. The river suddenly determines to shift its channel; the change may mean the destruction of a city, or a levee costing many thousands of dollars and months of labor to build. The engineers learn of the peril, and like firemen, hurry to the scene. They decide that only one of their giant mats will check the threatened diversion; soon after some monstrous vessels lumber down the water and tie up at the bank. This is the mat-plant, a black island of interlocked barges, so vast it seems impossible it is floating; it is a world of its own without boundaries.

Everywhere along the river grow the willows whose branches have a long life when completely submerged in water. With the arrival of the mat-plant, swarms of laborers go out and cut down these swift-growing trees by the thousands. Snorting steam cranes bring them to a barge on which is built a huge loom that weaves a carpet of incredible proportions—three hundred feet in width and sometimes a mile long. The hands of a thousand black and white laborers snatch up the slender trees and lay them out in regular patterns, while other hands wind in and out binding the wood with long strands of wire. Stocky white foremen stand everywhere; high above them all, like an old-time motion picture director, the superintendent sits in a little cabin built on a raised platform, watching the vast pageant unfolding before him, and calling his commands through a loud speaker instead of a megaphone. Soon a wide section of the green carpet is completed. The man in the cabin gives a signal. There is a hissing of steam and a creaking of cables. The great loom backs away from the carpet it has just created, and letting it drop to the river, goes on weaving a new half acre.

In the daylight, negroes come with wheelbarrows. Chanting rhythmically, they carry masses of stone from a barge moored alongside, and pile them on the wooden fabric floating in the river, till at last the balance is passed, and the great mat sinks below the surface, to lie along the sloping shore and the muddy bottom as a bulwark against the water's ravages.

I was visiting a mat-plant one afternoon when to my surprise I saw Ratty Joe of the snag boats, working with a crew of white men where the steam cranes were dropping their great loads of willows thunderously onto the deck.

"I've done come over for a little change," he explained as he took a huge chew of tobacco. "Get tired of snagging once in a while and get me a job here. It's like going to a big town, I reckon—so many people. I ain't never been to New York, but it's pretty near the same, everybody says. Something going on every minute. And there's always some mighty funny fellows. There's a nigger preacher here goes around with a axe hitting the other niggers on the head so they'll pray. And there's a white man on a mat up the river has a couple of pet crows the farmers along the bank are always wanting to buy. He waits till he's getting ready to move, and then he sells 'em. And next morning, when the boat is way down the river, here come the crows a-flying back to him, straight as a bee for a bobcat."

He spat with thoughtful accuracy at a little green turtle swimming down the water. "But I reckon the funniest one I knowed was a country fellow come from Arkansas was so green if you laid him on the grass you couldn't have seen him. He had rheumatism kind of bad and somebody told him if he'd catch a frog and wear it on a string like a watch, it'd take up all the rheumatism, and when the frog died he'd be well. So he done it, and wore the frog in his shirt pocket, and every minute he'd take it out and study it, like it was a watch sure enough and he was looking at the time of day. I

Mat Worker

reckon he wanted to see if it was getting thinner. But that there frog pretty near wrecked the mat plant. Every night all the moccasins in the swamp 'd come to the fellow's bed after the frog, and then they started coming in the daytime, too. It got so you couldn't pick up a cup of coffee at the table without a moccasin sitting there, getting mad if you didn't give him half. The boss made the fellow give the frog away."

The housing for the men of the mat plants is on the same vast scale as their labors. They live in enormous vessels known as quarter boats, two-storied structures several hundred feet long, like an army barracks devoid of its luxuries, with sleeping quarters expressively known to their black and white tenants as the bull pen. With their extraordinary fondness for nicknames, the negroes have aptly christened each huge building. The boat housing the executives is known as "the Sharp End"; the dormitory of the white workmen is called "Egg Shell"; while the giant home of the negroes themselves is known simply as "Black Bottom."

Since the quarter boats are the property of the Government, no gambling or drinking is permitted within their confines. But the shore is near and the land is free; within a few days of a quarter boat's establishment in the deepest wilderness, a thriving little town of camp followers will spring up along the bank. Hopefully in their tents and shacks and shantyboats the proprietors wait for the laborer's leisure and his payday; here the riverman can quickly lose all his money at cotch or coon-can and poker, or spend it on the gay-clad damsel who serves him his beer. In a few months the work is done, and the ponderous fleet moves on to a new field of endeavor. The dwellers on the shore pack up their gaming tables and their whisky and follow the watery trail.

There is a legend about one shrewd contractor years ago who was drowning in a sea of debts when he chanced to see a fortune in these tent towns of the camp followers. The contracts for the river projects at times are given to private corporations which make the most favorable bid; winning one of these contracts by far underbidding his competitors, he managed to borrow $6,000, enough to pay off his laborers for a week, then set up a score of gambling shacks on the bank. Late Friday afternoon was payday, and his paymasters carefully counted out the money into the laborers' hands. In a few moments there was an endless line going up to play at cards or dice, for his crew, like most rivermen, were inveterate gamblers; by Saturday morning almost every penny of the money was safely back in the company treasury. Each week the process was repeated. The contractor died a millionaire.

The engineers on the Mississippi possess little of the formality so often associated with the military, a quality which rests badly with the free and easy riverman. Occasionally, however, some general comes on from Washington for a technical inspection; and the strain on the rivermen in the engineers' employ may prove disastrous.

"I was captain on a snag boat once," my steamboat friend, Captain Bob, long retired from the service, related as we sat in a quiet New Orleans café drinking Sazeracs. "And we got word that some general who was one of the big bosses was on his way from the East. We got busy, and pretty soon we had that snag boat shining till you could have shaved in front of every table top or brass doorknob on her. Well, the general arrived, and we brought him to the boat. And I was sure glad we'd got everything fixed up, because you could see by looking at him he was one of those fussy ones. He was wearing civilian clothes, and he looked like a fashion plate. Hair slicked down and a polished moustache. You could see right away he was a big man with the ladies. He was wearing a beautiful suit, must have cost a million dollars, he said he just got in London. It was light gray, and looked like it just came out the store window—pressed to kill, and not a crease on it anywhere. He loved that suit like a woman does a new baby. First thing I tried to get him to take it off, because snagging's pretty rough work. But he wouldn't listen. For a couple of days everything went along fine. But the third day we struck a bad snag wouldn't come up with anything we tried. I saw the general watching, so I told the mate I'd fix it mighty quick, and I planted twelve sticks of dynamite on it, enough to blow that snag into sawdust and twenty others besides. And then I set it off."

Captain Bob sipped his Sazerac in reminiscence. "It didn't go off the first time, so I set it off again. There was a noise like Judgment Day, and then trees and logs began dropping everywhere out of the sky onto the boat. The deck smashed in, and the next thing I saw was the smokestacks falling into the river, and the smoke and soot was rolling out of the holes where they'd been like those oil fires you see in Texas. I looked for the general and didn't see him at first. But when I did, I wished I hadn't looked. His face was so black with soot, you'd have sworn he was a nigger, and that beautiful gray suit he bought in London was like a rag a cook uses to wipe off a greasy stove. We were way out in a wild part of the country, where we couldn't get any repairs, so for three days we had to go on with that smoke and soot blackening up everybody day and night till you couldn't have told your own brother, and the general staying locked up in his cabin, and having his meals brought in to him like he was in a jail. Some of the engineers told me for pretty near a year after he got back to his fancy parties in Washington, every time he shook hands with a lady he'd leave a black print."

But perhaps the most important labor of the engineers, and that which most obviously affects the lives of those many millions who inhabit the vast regions of interior America, is the work of flood control. The source of much of the flood problem goes back to human greed and selfishness. A farmer with some rich bottom land would grow tired of watching his acres flood each year with the approach of spring, and would build an earthen wall a few feet high to keep out the onrushing waters; his neighbor, seeing the success of the plan, would set up a similar wall. The idea spread like a contagious disease, and crossed the water to the opposite shore. Natural outlets to the Gulf were barricaded. Soon the river was enclosed in two great walls running with only an occasional gap from the cities and cornfields of Missouri to the pungent French market in New Orleans and beyond. Factories and parks and the draining of swamps lessened still further those areas which had been the natural drainage basins of the river, into which it could pour when over-burdened. The rivermen, foreseeing the future, protested; the answer of the towns and farmers was to build the levees higher. When the floods arrived it was exactly as though a municipal water works for the sake of economy suddenly decided to force a six-inch stream of water through a three-inch pipe; somewhere a break was certain.

The great flood of 1927, with its appalling loss of life and property, taught the valley its lesson. The engineers decided to restore to the river some of its long-lost freedom. The

levees are far back from the stream now; here and there are fuse plugs, wide safety gates which can be opened and allow the waters to spill over vast areas of swamp, to the discomfiture of only the raccoons and the wildcats compelled to seek a drier home. And occasionally the engineers cut through the great loops of the river, so that the flood waters can speed swiftly down the shortened channel and disappear beyond the Jetties in the blue Gulf.

The building of one of the levees, like the making of the mats, is an impressive pageant in black and white moving against the yellow of the valley clay. Everywhere are negroes and whites, toiling with shovels or driving sweating mules; beyond them the giant steam diggers clank and whine as they open their great jaws hungrily and bury their teeth in the crumbling ground. Each day the earthen wall grows higher and higher, twisting through the cypress woods like some gigantic serpent seeking its prey. Most of the levees have been the work of private companies, with the engineers merely making the plans and watching their execution. The labor was hard, and men at times difficult to obtain; as a result, the levee camp was often known as a sort of Foreign Legion of the Mississippi, a refuge where the fugitive from the law would be sheltered in peace and anonymity.

"There's sure been some mighty bad people working on the levees," Jack of Diamonds, the fat cook of one of the camps told me, as he stood preparing some meat cakes for the workers' supper. "Worst fellow I ever knowed in 'em anywheres was a big nigger named Cotton. Cotton done killed fifty niggers, I reckon, and every time he killed a new one he come to the levee camp and the boss always took him in. The detectives never could catch him. And even if he was in a camp where the boss didn't know him, and would have give him to the law, didn't make no difference. He'd jest wake up all of a sudden in the middle of the night, and rub his head kind of funny with his hand and say 'My head's hot. They're coming for me. I got to git away.' And he'd put on his hat and his pants and be out in them swamps and gone. Next day some detectives 'd come in, and ask us where Cotton was, and then run out with some big bloodhounds, yelling and hollering. I knowed it was a mojo he done it with, was give to him by a old woman in Natchez. And one night he showed it to me. It was a little dead man jest as big as your finger, laying in a little coffin, and dressed in the prettiest suit you ever seen."

He put the meat cakes one by one on the huge stove. "I got a pretty good mojo, too. It's a powder I puts on the doorknob so when the landlord comes to git the rent from my wife in Greenville, he touches it and forgits all about what he come for. I ain't paid no rent for a year. But I'd sure like to have that mojo against them detectives."

It is during the great floods which sweep down in the springtime and test the levees to the breaking point that the work of the engineers reaches its peak. With the valley become a vast sea lapping higher and higher at the protecting walls of the towns till they seem like beleaguered, vanishing islands, the engineers toil hour after hour without ceasing. Now they rush to pile sandbags where a crack threatens in the weakened earth; now they build a mudbox filled with earth along the top of the levee to make it rise a few feet higher against the attacking river. Sleepless, they help the natives organize their levee guard; for a levee, despite its vastness, is a fragile thing in high water, and two reckless, invading farmers, anxious to deflect the flood from the opposite shore, can use a piece of barbed wire as a saw, and make a cut that in a few hours will become a raging Niagara. Each engineer boat is a messenger of mercy, dashing out over the raging waters to succor the sick and rescue the drowning from the trees or the submerging rooftops; crowded with refugees, in a few brief hours their crews witness the complete cycle of life from birth to death, and see enacted before them all the extremes of joy and tragedy in the drama that is human existence.

They are humble souls, these natives of the Valley, who know like the dwellers on Vesuvius that they are ever at the mercy of the great force which encircles their lives. And like them, the engineers are humble men as well. It is their hope, and the hope of the inhabitants with them, that the cut-offs, and the fuse-plugs, and the mats, and the new levees, will avert all the normal floods that assail the banks and send the muddy waters harmlessly on their way to join the ocean. Each day they wage their relentless war against the river; but they realize only too well that their science and their guile, and their dredge boats and their survey boats are after all but a brave pretense; in the end they can only urge and persuade. Deep in their hearts they know that on the day when the Ohio, and the Tennessee, and the Cumberland, and the Upper Mississippi, and the Missouri, and the St. Francis, and the White and the Black and the Green and the Red, all chance to overflow their banks in a vast and simultaneous inundation as some great storm sweeps between the mountains on the East and on the West, there is no human power which can predict the swirling water's course or check catastrophe. For though man with his learning may in quieter moments seem to exercise a slight control over the great forces of Nature, let those forces rise in their wrath, and he becomes as a helpless child struggling in the darkness of infinity.

The technical head of the engineers is a stately official in some white marbled palace in Washington. But every riverman and every engineer knows that the real power who in the end directs their destinies is the great alligator who sits on his throne deep down in the mud of the bottom, and with his huge paw scoops up a new sandbar to block the channel or with a lash of his long tail sends a levee toppling into the yellow water. Year after year he sits, temperamental, unpredictable, one moment generously endowing the shores along his course with golden richness, the next raging in fury and whipping them off to destruction, while packet-boats, towboats, shantymen, shoremen, wait upon each changing whim.

For one cannot really argue with royalty. And this is Old Al, the River King.

U. S. Willow

V

RIVER LIGHT

FROM history's earliest beginnings, when the skin-clad
native woman stood by the sea with a flaming torch
waiting for the return of her mate, the traveler on the water,
whether it be fresh or salt, has regarded the light that guided
him to the shore with a deep reverence that was almost wor-
ship. And with reason. I have lived in Africa beneath the
old Carthaginian lighthouse that guided Hannibal's galleys
up the blue bay of Tunis. I have watched the twinkling bea-
cons of Havre, and Brest, and Plymouth, and Sandy Hook.
I have steamed past the lights glowing with a pale yellow
flame at the edge of some reeking cypress swamp of the

Mississippi. And everywhere there was a sense of the hidden, the mysterious. The lighthouse of Sandy Hook and the lighthouse at Tunis are known to a myriad travelers; but though there is scarcely a person of the millions dwelling in the great Mississippi Valley who, when driving near the water, has not seen the river lights flickering sadly in the distance, to no one but the rivermen have they any meaning. These lights and their lightkeepers are unknown stars and shadows in a little-known world, the world of the river.

From the bustling cities of St. Paul and Minneapolis, where the blinker lights flash in brilliant rhythm, to the green jetties far below New Orleans where a drowsy pelican sits on the post beside each polished lamp, the river lights mount their guard to protect the passing vessels from disaster. Their very names are touched with the strange and the bizarre—Hanging Dog Light, Dark Slough Light, Devil's Island Float Light; they are rich calendars of local history and legend. The lighthouse service everywhere on the Mississippi is a thing of fascination; but the section of the river where the life of the lightkeeper goes on in the leisurely fashion of the olden days, unaffected by the turmoil of an ever-changing world, is the lower river between Memphis and New Orleans. Here cities and towns are infrequent and factories almost non-existent; there are only sunless woods and tangled swamps where long cranes fly like wandering ghosts and alligators crawl silently. Here there are no blinker lights powered by electricity; here there are only coal-oil lamps burning like the lights of those times far in the past when the boats of today were unborn.

A river light possesses an importance that no mere land dweller can even faintly measure. It may mean life or death to a crew; it may mean the saving or destruction of a million-dollar cargo. I have been a cub pilot at night when a sudden fog descended, and I have stood beside the steersman, peering blindly ahead, while the vessel beneath us floundered helpless in the gray maze. And I know that feeling of exaltation when a spectral blur appeared faintly over the bow, that meant we had found the light we were seeking.

The lightkeeper knows his importance as well as the pilot. He knows that he has only one task: whatever the risk, he must make his way to the pole where a great brass lamp rests on a wooden bracket, and keep the light burning.

The perils of the lightkeeper's life are many. Though the wind is blowing a hurricane lashing the river into mountainous waves that overwhelm his frail skiff and each instant threaten to capsize it; though a flood is raging, with wrecked houses, timbers, and broken bridges sweeping swiftly down upon him, he does not hesitate. Though the mist is so thick he cannot see the oars in his hands, he must grope his way across the river in constant terror of being crushed by the barges of some lost towboat.

But his greatest enemy is the caving bank, a perpendicular wall sometimes seventy or eighty feet high, on top of which his light is resting. As he moors his rowboat below he must watch with all the vigilance of an Alpine climber expecting an avalanche, lest the great cliff suddenly topple and bury him alive. Many a keeper has died in this fashion, with only the crew of the lighthouse tender and the superintendent in far off St. Louis to know of his heroism.

The courage and devotion of the lightkeepers is shared by their children. When the father grows too old and the mother is feeble as well, the son or the daughter assumes the responsibility. Near Natchez there lived such a child, Lutey May, a beautiful, flaxen-haired little girl who had taken over the duties of her sick mother, and was the darling of all the pilots who passed. Then one spring, there came a high flood that washed out the lights everywhere. It tore away Lutey May's light as well. But the child did not falter. Calmly she took the extra lantern which the Government men had supplied her, and hung it in a tree near the water where the light had been standing. Each day, though the river here was particularly dangerous, she went out to trim the wick and fill the reservoir. The flood continued for weeks, and the pilots, the most sentimental and the kindliest of men, nodded their heads in pride. Then one pilot of my acquaintance purchased a basket of the fanciest fruits he could find in Natchez, and sent them by an old negro lounging on the wharf to the dilapidated little cabin that Towhead called her home. An hour later the negro returned, his wrinkled face gray, his hand still holding the basket.

The pilot looked at him in wonder. "What you brought that basket back for, Uncle Lace?" he demanded. "You going crazy or something? I told you to take it to the house and leave it."

The old negro shook his snowy head and mumbled in apology. "I sure couldn't leave it, Capt'n," he said. "She done went out to fix her light and a bank caved in and she done got drowned. The preacher and the undertaker they was all in the house a-waiting for 'em to find her in the river. I seen her mother a-sitting there and I give her the fruit, like you said. But I don't know, seemed like she didn't want it someways. It's sure mighty pretty fruit, Capt'n."

Besides caving banks and floods, the keeper has other, lesser enemies. There are the willow bugs, great blundering creatures, who live just long enough to drop into a light, and cause the glass to become smoky and dull. There are human enemies as well. There is the coon hunter, who, when out in the swamp, finds there is no more oil in the miner's lamp he is wearing on his cap, and replenishes his supply at the Government light, as a traveler fills his fountain pen in the writing room of a hotel. Worst of all there is the moonshiner, who discovers that he has brought insufficient fuel for his bubbling mash, and considering his need greater than that of the passing steamboats, empties the reservoir of the lamp into his oil can and carries it away to his still.

"They sure got mighty fine coal oil in them Government lights," the overalled swamp dweller will confide as he sets out some jugs of his product for an expected customer. "Government always gets the best there is."

These latter practices are growing rare, however, for the

Secret Service agents have been vigorous, and the too-casual
woodsmen are in the penitentiary, pondering over the error
of their ways.

For in difficult sections of the river, the lack of a light or
the mistaking of a light is almost certain to end in tragedy.
Though occasionally the results may be humorous instead.

"Funny thing happened round here a couple of years ago,"
drawled the drowsy-eyed Sandbar Jack as he poured some
oil into the reservoir and shined the brass bowl. "A pilot got
mixed up on a light at Ash Creek and quicker than a bee
sting the boat was stuck on a bar. Bad luck for the pilot, it
was mighty late in the spring, and the water was a-dropping
terrible fast. It kept on a-dropping till the boat was out of
water like she was the Ark on Ararat. And pretty soon she
was half a mile from the river, with the squirrels and chip-
munks a-playing on her paddle wheel. When it got thataway, the captain and the crew all left her, and wasn't nobody
stayed behind except the engineer to keep up steam, Big Sam,
I reckon you know him, comes from up White River way.
Big Sam had a mighty nice time, talking to me and the other
fishermen around here, and a-hollering and a-joking at all the
boats went past, and a-drawing his salary all the time. But
pretty soon he got tired, and he said he was a country boy
anyways and always wanted a farm when he got off the river,
so he figured he'd plant him a potato crop. A farmer around
here give him some seed potatoes, and Big Sam planted 'em
right by the rudder of the boat. Any time of day you'd pass
there you'd see him a-working, hoeing, and turning the
ground, a-watching the river all the time, hoping she
wouldn't come up till he got his crop done. And then Fall
come, and he dug up his potatoes, and they was the finest
ever seen in the Valley. Big as punkins and sweeter than

sugar cane. Eating one of them potatoes was like eating a bag of marshmallows. Next day after he had 'em all in, the river come up and floated the boat away."

With all its responsibilities and perils, the task of lightkeeper is one of the prizes of the river. For not only does it invest the holder of the post with the dignity of the Government—and there is no more ardent patriot than the riverman—but it provides him as well with a regular income of ten dollars a month for each light that he tends. And on the river where life is simple and money is rare, ten dollars is many times that sum in a great metropolis. In consequence, lights remain in the same family for generations; the waiting list is long and the jealousies intense. More than once a lightkeeper has started on his daily round to find that his flatboat has been smashed with an ax during the night; or he has rowed a little way across the river only to find the water pouring through a half dozen leaks in the bottom of his boat where the seams have been carefully parted, and he has been compelled to swim for his life. More than one keeper has been found killed in some mysterious fashion; and all the Valley knows that an envious neighbor seeking his lights has been the murderer.

As the years pass, often a good keeper may acquire other lights, sometimes ten, even fifteen, and here he rises to the status of a merchant prince, a veritable captain of industry. And if, by some accident of fate, this fortunate individual should be a woman, she becomes a queen, to be assiduously wooed by all her male neighbors of the river, anxious to acquire a wealthy wife. They are excellent lightkeepers, the women, at times superior to the men, worried if a speck or smear mars the lamp's spotless surface.

The life of the lightkeeper is a happy one, filled with infinite variety. When his duties are not pressing he can go out to fish in his pirogue, a dugout made of a single log, unchanged since the days of the Indians. He can chew tobacco and talk all day with the crews of the towboats who have come into shore to remake their tows, or philosophize with the Government men. He may hear of some unfortunate drowned on a picnic up the river, and with his rowboat ready, will keep close watch of the passing drift. There will be a knock on his door, and it may be a neighbor come to bring him a wild turkey; or it may be a grim figure with hair clipped short and face scratched with briars, an escaped convict come to demand at pistol point that he be rowed to the dismal swamp visible on the other shore. Life is full of adventure and uncertainty.

The ordinary lightkeeper is a white fisherman. But there are a few who depart from the pattern. There are a score of negroes, all excellent keepers, and even a Filipino. Some of the keepers live in shantyboats anchored near their lights, some in shantyboats beached on the shore. A few live in Choctaws, houses built on great hollow logs so that when the high water comes the curious structures float off with no damage to the interior, and as the yellow flood slowly recedes, the occupants can set them down again wherever they will. One lightkeeper operates a little sawmill; one has a shantyboat store where he sells candy and pop to passing river travelers; another, whose lights are all on one side of the water, is the possessor of an old and faithful horse, and every day rides out with his lamps and supplies dangling from the animal's sides.

They number some picturesque characters. There is the Skipper, an amiable giant tanned by the sun to the color of an Indian, who was once a schoolteacher. Seized with the

spell of the river, he began spending all his holidays at the
water's edge, talking with the boatmen and the shantymen;
when the lightkeepers fell ill, occasionally in kindliness he
tended their lamps. Time passed, and the confinement of
the schoolhouse grew less and less attractive. At last he abandoned the classroom and his comfortable home in the city
to live in the peace of the river wilderness, a keeper now with
his own lights, watching the fish leap in silvery arcs from the
water, or a great hoot owl fly against the moon. And there is
of course Sandbar Jack, who lives in a shantyboat beneath
some cottonwoods and has a moth-eaten dog named Preacher
who is his soul and life. Sometimes a visitor arrives to find
Preacher whimpering and tugging miserably at the end of
a rusty chain; Sandbar Jack quickly announces the reason.

"That there Preacher's a wonderful dog," he drawls, as he
leans to caress the animal's woebegone head. "He's about the
finest blooded dog between here and New Orleans, I reckon.

Maybe up to St. Paul, too, but he ain't been up that way. If I could just git him off to a show, I'd sure make a pile of money. But he's the running-awayest dog I ever seen. I got him tied up now 'cause I just give him a trial, judge, and jury, and everything—it was me and some of the shantymen around here—and we done sentenced him to ten days on the chain gang. He's served two of 'em now. And he don't like it no-ways. If he runs away again, the jury's going to sentence him to thirty days, they says."

Whatever the lightkeeper may be, shantyman or land dweller, there is one important day in his life, the day of the arrival of the lighthouse boat. For the lighthouse boat is the keeper's link with the outside world, and its whistle the beginning and end of his calendar. There are a number of lighthouse boats, all picturesque, that ply the northern river and the tributaries, like the sturdy *Greenbrier* captained by my boyhood friend Red, that voyages up the Ohio and the winding Tennessee. Each of these vessels is the monarch of its own watery kingdom. The proud mistress of the lights of the lower river is the white and shining *Willow*, with the gentle, soft-spoken Captain Bernard at the wheel that guides her on her way.

The *Willow* is a side-wheeler, one of the few remaining on the river, and is built like a battleship to resist the storms and floods that Old Al, the river god, sends against her. The master of the *Willow*, and the other lighthouse boats, must be far more than a pilot. He must be doctor, engineer, lawyer, draftsman, midwife, preacher, and a diplomat fit for service in a foreign land. For he must concern himself not only with all the usual worries of a steamboat captain, its operation, its fuel bills, the troubles of his crew, but he must be intimately concerned with the life of every lightkeeper along the bank. He must cure them when they are sick, free them from jail when they have run afoul of the sheriff, bury them when they are dead. And just as the captain must be a man of many talents, so must the crew. Not only must they be steamboaters, but they must be expert carpenters, swiftly able to fashion the wooden standards that form the lights' support; they must be expert laddermen, who can climb a seventy-foot perpendicular bank ready to collapse upon them at any moment with the speed and skill of firemen mounting the wall of a blazing factory.

The caving bank is the enemy of the individual light-keeper. But it is the curse, the consummation of all evil for the *Willow*. The individual lightkeeper has only one cav-ing bank to battle; the *Willow's* life is a voyage from one land-slide to another, each worse than the last. All day long her crew are setting up their tall ladders; all day the captain scans the horizon with his field glasses to see if the light ahead has toppled into the river. Then he sees a telltale circle of milky foam on the water. And he sighs, for he knows that a bank is caving again.

Even the riverman who has been acquainted since his earliest days with the habits of the Mississippi, and knows how overnight it can change its course so that a city on its shore will be suddenly twenty miles inland, never ceases to be astonished at the stream's grim restlessness. It is this con-tinuous change, this unceasing attack upon its banks, which occasions so much of the *Willow's* labor. The vessel will start from Cairo and set all the lights two hundred and fifty feet from the bank, safe from the water's ravages; by the time it has reached Baton Rouge and started up the river again, scores of the lights will have vanished completely, and a myriad others will be at the water's edge, ready to dive like their fellows into extinction.

They are appalling spectacles, these caving banks, with great oaks and cypresses tossing about like toy trees in a child's fairy forest, and whole plains breaking, like the world's end.

As they are expert laddermen, so must the *Willow's* crew be superlative woodsmen, for in a flash they must clear away the edge of an obscuring forest so that the lamp will be visible in all directions. For a single light I have seen them compelled to cut three hundred trees. For the smaller undergrowth the boat itself is sometimes used as the axman, a great loop of rope being circled around the brush and saplings to be cleared, while the other end of the line is made fast to the prow. The captain, waiting in the pilot house, signals the engine room. With an explosive crackling of branches the boat begins to back away; in a moment the bank is level as a prairie and a mound of broken willows is floating down the river.

It is during these timber-cutting operations that some of the more amusing phases of the *Willow's* colorful life come into evidence. A hornet's nest on a tree or a light post calls for much consultation and strategy among the negro roustabouts, occasionally ending in rout and a panic-struck run down the bank. Or Hominy, a lean, thoughtful negro who is the boat's champion snake smeller, will look gravely about him, and say, "I smells a snake." And the search for the reptile is instantly begun.

"I can smell 'em every time," Hominy will tell you in his leisure moments of the evening, as he sits chewing a green gumdrop from the bag some friend ashore has provided. "They smells jest like a watermelon. Guess that's kind of

right for them to be thataway. Watermelon and water moccasin, they both got plenty of water in 'em. But it ain't the
water moccasins I'm worst scared of. It's them blowing vipers
that's the bad ones. They'll jest sit around a light a-waiting
for you to come, and the minute they see you they blows a
cloud of smoke at you, jest like it was coming out of a chimney, only blue. And if you git jest one of them blue smells,
you drop dead right where you're standing. I reckon you
seen all them yellow leaves on them cottonwoods up at Scrub
Grass Bend Light this morning. Them leaves was all killed
by smoke from a blowing viper."

The study of unnatural natural history is as intense among
the roustabouts of the *Willow* as on any other Mississippi
steamboat, perhaps more so because of the vessel's govern-
mental and thus educational character. I chanced to witness
one extraordinary demonstration. The solemn Hominy declared one evening that a frog would smoke a cigarette, and
when the white members of the crew grew ribald, hurried
ashore, and returned bearing a frog in his long black fingers.
Borrowing a cigarette from one of the spectators, he lit it
carefully and inserted the other end into the frog's thin
mouth. The frog seemed to stare at this unexpected gift in
surprise a moment, then settled down to a long smoke with
all the apparent luxurious enjoyment of an old soldier for
weeks deprived of his tobacco. Suddenly it gave a gulp, and
before any of the astonished spectators could prevent, swallowed the half consumed cigarette, with the end still glowing redly like a beacon on the shore. It seemed to suffer no
ill effects from the unusual diet, for several of the crew kept
anxious watch over the little animal in a soap box transformed into the observation ward of a hospital. But it continued sprightly and agile as ever, hopping gaily over the

decks whenever it was released from confinement, until at last, satisfied, its nurses let it go merrily bounding up the bank again.

"Them frogs 'll smoke a cigarette every time," Hominy remarked gravely as he watched it disappear in the crackling brush. "I've had a big bullfrog pretty near pull a cigarette out of my hand plenty of times. And talk about 'em eating fire. I used to live on a plantation down near Greenville where there was a heap of frogs. And when I'd go out to empty the ashes from the stove, frogs 'd come from everywhere and jump up and git all the red-hot coals from the pan before they hit the ground. It's cause a frog was born inside a fire. That there's wrote in the Bible."

The whistle on the *Willow* is a treasured heirloom. It was the whistle of the *Oleander,* which before the days of the *Willow* moved slowly up the water from flickering light to flickering light; when in the distant future the *Willow* goes off to the paradise of good steamboats, the whistle will be lifted down tenderly and set up over the gleaming deck of a new vessel waiting to start on its adventurous career. So beloved is this whistle, lightkeepers have solemnly declared that if by some chance it were ever changed, they would refuse to answer the strange call and would resign their posts.

All men aboard a river vessel live in close association; on the *Willow,* they become members of a friendly family. The boat is away from her port for months, and must take the place of the homes of which the crew are deprived in their enforced wanderings. The family life that in a household centers about the living room on the boat is concentrated in the cabin. Here the holidays are celebrated; here Christmas becomes a gay festivity. A Christmas tree is set up, and Spanish moss from the swamps is hung from the ceiling. Paper flowers are tacked on the walls, and everywhere there are Christmas stockings for the keepers. And as the *Willow* remembers these sturdy guardians of the river, so do the keepers never forget the *Willow*. There are presents for the crew of great bags of pecans and wild honey from the forest; there are rabbits, and giant catfish, and beautiful fishing poles made from the swaying cane that grows along the shore.

I have chanced to be aboard when some of the poorer of these river dwellers first saw the white-painted interior of the *Willow,* with its windows where no glass is broken, and its roof without a crack, and their faces were a study in the degrees of human ecstasy. One evening a mother and child who lived in a bare little cabin on the bank walked timidly up the gangplank for a visit. For several moments the woman stood in awed silence, gazing at the immaculate cabin with its long table set with shining dishes and a white napkin

folded neatly at each place. Then her eyes grew wistful. "I ain't seen nothing like this since I been in the hospital," she said.

The lives of the crew of the *Willow,* like the lives of the lightkeepers, are often troubled, and full of peril. They are pioneers; they must take the risks so that others may follow. Rarely are they near a town where they can enjoy the pleasures of the world outside to which they were once accustomed; when they tie up at night it is near a light in some tangled wilderness, with the cry of the wildcat their only company. Yet their life has many compensations. They know the secrets of the swamps, the ways of the muskrat, the coon, the wily panther. And the pageant of the river is always passing before them.

One day they will see two dogs drowning in a swift current, and set out swiftly in the yawl to effect their rescue, only to find that when the animals are brought dripping aboard, they fight desperately with tooth and claw until they are put ashore. And next morning the crew learns the dogs were in no danger. The animals were crossing the river for their daily call on a shantyman who served his canine friends a five o'clock tea each afternoon, and they were properly indignant at the interruption to their social calendar.

On another day the boat may pass an old fort along the river, and if it is twilight, when the swamp birds flap their great wings somberly over the cypresses, and ghosts fly softly behind them, the crew can hear the sound of bugles and the galloping hoofs of cavalry still re-echoing from a bitter-fought battle of the Civil War.

There is a tranquillity in the life of the lighthouse boat and the keepers that breeds a rich mellowness and kindliness. A cutoff in the river may eliminate the light of a faithful tender and threaten him with the loss of the monthly ten dollars which is his very existence; the captain of the lighthouse boat tries to find some other light near by and avoid a tragedy. For the lighthouse service is loyal to its loyal servants.

Some years ago up one of the small tributaries a group of pilots came to the captain of the lighthouse tender in the region, and asked that a light be moved from one side of the river to the other. The bank and the channel had changed, they declared, and the light must be placed on the other shore, if their labors were not to be increased tenfold and their vessels even wrecked.

The captain of the lighthouse boat, an old man grown gray at his post became troubled. "I'll move her for you next week," he declared. "But I'm sure mighty sorry it's got to go. That light's kept by Aunt Mollie Snow, that's been having it for forty years, ever since her husband drowned going out to fix his lamp. The light money's all she's got to support herself and two grandchildren. I don't think she'll ever be able to cross the river. She's too twisted up with rheumatism. I reckon she'll just have to lose it, that's all."

The pilots went away, looking worried. They returned the next morning. "Captain, we don't want that light changed at Greenpoint," said the spokesman. "We'll get along fine with the light where she is. Pilots can just be kind of extra careful going round her."

The captain of the lighthouse boat smiled, and nodded.

And the light remained until Aunt Mollie was dead.

For this is the code of the river.

Big Business

VI

BARGE LINE

ALONG the Mississippi two columns of black smoke are arising, twin symbols of a force that is changing the destiny of all interior America. These columns of smoke are vitally affecting every city and town along the river that is the great artery through which pours the life blood of the nation; they symbolize a force which touches towns far up the fog-tipped Alleghenies in the east, and at the edges of the snowy Rockies to the west.

The twin columns of smoke are steamboat smoke; the

force they symbolize is the towboat of the barge lines, which is remaking the map of the nation.

The towboat has existed on the Mississippi from long before the time I can remember, when as a boy I used to sit on the river bank and watch the long tows of coal go drifting down the water to far-off New Orleans. But it is only in the last ten years that it has reached the status of a vast new industry. Every American who has ever gazed upon one of those vivid colored lithographs of the *Robt. E. Lee* and the *Natchez* racing down the river, with towering flames leaping from their stacks, knows that the packet boats with their chanting roustabouts in the olden days carried vast quantities of freight over the yellow water; none but rivermen know it is because of the towboat that today the Mississippi and its tributaries are bearing more freight than at any time since steamboating began. On a single river, the Monongahela, more freight is carried by the towboats plying between the steel mills of Pittsburgh and the rich coal mines of Pennsylvania than passes through the giant Panama Canal; so important has river navigation become that a plant at Pittsburgh engaged in building riverboats, in a year constructed more vessels than all but one of the great shipyards situated along the nation's seacoasts. Because of the towboat with its cheap transportation, new factories are moving in a hurried procession to the water fronts. Towns that were famous river ports are in the mouths of boatmen once more: Kansas City, St. Paul, Memphis, New Orleans. The Mississippi Valley is booming.

The towboat of the barge lines which has brought about these changes, is closely related to the packet boat, now almost a vanished American. Most of the towboats are still stern-wheelers, and much resemble the older vessels; but some of the lines have committed the mortal sin of building craft with propellers like ocean boats, an act which, certain river veterans insist, will some day result in their rotting in the mud of the river bottom, dragged down by Old Al, the river king.

They are giants, these towboats, and as they move in dignity up and down the water, they push in the long barges clustered around their prows the equivalent of sixteen loaded freight trains. They are built of steel; they may be huge vessels costing half a million dollars and with engines possessing the strength of three thousand horses, the power of many an ocean-going vessel; they may be equipped with radio and every convenience known to the age. Yet despite these changes, towboating has lost little of its picturesqueness; the post of towboat pilot demands all its former alertness and skill. The pilot of a packet boat had a vessel to steer that reached to a length of perhaps three hundred feet; the towboat pilot must direct a craft that with the ten or fifteen barges lying before him may stretch out beyond a thousand feet, the length of a great ship on the ocean. The packet pilot steers a boat; the tow pilot guides a floating world. To anyone who has seen the Mississippi in the low water of summer, when the river becomes a Sahara-like desert with only the merest thread of water trickling through the middle, navigating a tow a quarter of a mile long in and out the maze of sand bars waiting to entrap it, becomes a miracle almost comparable to piloting the *Queen Mary* down the narrow twisting streets of the East End of London after a light spring rain.

The packet boat is like a fast, graceful racehorse, who can ford a stream, or climb a mountain at will. The towboat is a pack horse, or an Arab donkey, loaded down until it seems his back must break under the burden. It must always seek the easiest road.

"Piloting a packet boat 'll turn a baby's hair gray," the vitriolic Captain Andy burst out, as he sent the immense tow before him around a snag thrusting its jagged head out of the water. "But piloting a towboat 'll drive you raving crazy. In low water you get stuck on the bottom every minute and go so slow the mosquitoes eat you alive; in high water, you keep close to shore to get an eddy to help you upstream, and then moccasins and rattlers drop on you from the trees. And when you come to the cutoffs the Government people's built so the flood water 'll run out faster to the Gulf, you can't go through 'em like any regular boat. The current's too fast for you and you have to go around."

He chewed his cud of tobacco angrily. "Look at me the last time I tried to get through one of the cutoffs. Didn't have such a big tow. Only eight pieces. And it sure cuts off plenty. Three quarters of a mile instead of twenty-one miles. I started through about breakfast time and then I found out

pretty quick I couldn't make it. Mate hadn't fixed the tow
up right, or something. I started the long way around the
bend, that's twenty-one miles, and going two miles an hour.
Couldn't make any more, 'cause the water was running pretty
fast. We traveled all day fighting her. I got round to the top
of the cutoff about supper time, and looked down and saw
the bottom where we were early in the morning, just three
quarters of a mile away. 'Well,' I said to Captain Jack, my
partner, who came in to relieve me. 'It's something to get
here anyway.' Just as I said it, the current in the cutoff got
the forward end of the barges. And before I could turn the
wheel, my whole tow was going down through the cutoff
like those streamlined trains go out of St. Louis. And in
about a minute we were at the bottom, right where we had
started. Then they wonder why steamboat men go to the
lunatic asylum."

It is the temperamental, highly individualistic quality of
the towboat pilot as well as that of the river itself which
gives towboating so much of its picturesqueness. For the
towboat man, like the sailor or the explorer close to the
elements and to life and death, remembers his philosophy
and his traditions. I have traveled on towboats equipped with
electrical loud speakers to carry the soundings from the distant prow of the barges to the pilot house. But the calls that
came over the loud speakers were not some clipped modern
phrases designed to fit this new ingenious instrument. They
were the same old calls that echoed over the water in the
days of Natchez under the Hill: the poignant No Bottom,
the melancholy Mark Tyree, the dreamy Quarter Less Twain.
There has been no change; no pilot has thought of changing.
For the towboat pilot like his brother the packet pilot, is
an artist, a poet, not a mere driver of an automobile who

can learn the trick in several weeks of practice. There have been a few towboat pilots who took to the wheel because it paid them a salary, like keeping books or working in a factory. But their careers on the river were brief and always ended in disaster.

The towboat pilot, like all other rivermen, is kindly and sentimental, ready to give his last penny or his life for a friend or a stray dog on the bank. Hour after hour he stands at the wheel, drinking his black coffee as in the olden days, joking, arguing, seemingly unconscious of his task, yet in reality always alert, and watching each line and shadow in the yellow stream that winds in ever changing pattern before him. And like the pilots of the olden days, he is apt to be fiery-tempered. The barges whine and moan as they rub against each other; continuing through the long watches of the night, the sound may fray the taut nerves of the steersman.

I was in the pilot house my first night aboard with the excitable Captain Andy, listening to the doleful wailing of the barges, when suddenly I heard him swear. A moment later he blew the whistle for the watchman.

"Get down there and fix those barges," he demanded explosively, when the lanky watchman known as Slim shambled through the door of the pilot house. "If they don't stop squealing, I'm going to cut 'em loose and let 'em go on down the river. Sounds like a farmer killing all his pigs."

Slim shrugged his lean shoulders. Slowly he went down the stairs and walked out into the blackness of the tow. A loud metallic clangor followed. Captain Andy nodded in satisfaction.

A little while later I met Slim in the cook's galley. He winked at me broadly. "Captain Andy's sure a card," he drawled, stuffing down a huge cheese sandwich. "I can't do nothing to them barges. Some of 'em you can fix with oil and wooden plugs. But this here kind is just natural hollering barges. So I just goes out and kind of drops a monkey wrench a few times and drag some tow chains over the deck. And Captain Andy thinks I'm a-working hard, and gets to feeling better. I been a-doing it for him every night going on to seven years."

It was a curious, almost fantastic combination of two widely separated events that brought about the present revival of the towboat, the first the cutting of the Panama Canal, the second the entrance of the United States into the World War. From long before the coming of Columbus, the Mississippi and its tributaries had been the highway of the Indians; since the beginning of time rivers have been the roads laid down by a generous Nature over which man might journey. After the Indians came the French explorers, still in canoes, then the rafts and the flatboats, manned by roaring, swashbuckling rivermen; after these came the first steamboats, rickety, rattletrap affairs, coughing smoke and soot everywhere. And wherever these boats shifted their cargoes, at a falls, or the mouth of a stream where they met other rivermen and sat around in some little tavern making desperate love to the barmaid, little settlements and towns began to appear. These towns grew and prospered, with the river front the center from which everything radiated. And the steamboats lying at the wharves were their life.

The steamboats grew in size and beauty until they were floating palaces.

Suddenly there developed another smoky machine that sputtered showers of sparks and clouds of soot from an odd-bellied smokestack, and ran over two strips of iron set on what appeared to be a row of matchsticks—the iron horse of the railroad. The iron horse rode further and further over the countryside. And as this curious monster stood smoking and panting along the banks of the Mississippi, he watched the graceful packet boats glide up and down the river with their cargoes, and decided that they must die.

The resolution thus made was quickly translated into action. Steamboat lines were bought only to be abandoned and the white painted vessels left rotting at the wharves. Freight rates were reduced to the vanishing point. So successful was the iron horse's campaign that as the years passed the seemingly endless lines of packets that had once plied the river shrunk to a few scattered vessels fighting desperately for their existence.

In 1914 the Panama Canal was built and a great change came over the Mississippi Valley. With the cutting of the Canal, the cities of the Valley were placed at a disadvantage so severe in some cases it proved fatal. The cities on the Atlantic and Pacific coasts could ship to each other by cheap water transportation through the Canal, and the railroads, to meet the competition, dropped their rates accordingly. But the inland cities were now deprived of their steamboats, and were compelled to pay the highest rates the successors of the clanking iron horse chose to demand. The disparity grew so enormous that a factory in New York could send a pair of shoes all the way to San Francisco for less money than a factory in St. Louis could ship the same pair of shoes a few miles by train.

The results were soon apparent. Factories began to leave the Valley, or if they did not depart entirely, erected new plants near the coasts, where with low rates they could compete for the commerce of the world. The cities near the oceans prospered. But the Valley, the center of so many of the nation's vital resources, languished.

It needed a World War to bring about the revolution. In 1918, as a military measure, the Government took over the railroads, and decided to help relieve the congestion by reviving the long forgotten waterways. Purchasing a tiny fleet of two towboats and nine barges already in erratic operation on the Missouri, officials started a service from St. Louis to New Orleans. A little later they opened another branch, on the Warrior River in Alabama, to carry the coal and iron of Birmingham off to the munition factories and the arsenals. When the war ended, the new lines would normally have ended as well. But the planters and the merchants and the industrialists of the Valley remembered their steamboats, and insisted that the plan be continued. Their pleas were heeded; the project was incorporated as a private company, with the Government owning all the stock, under the rolling title of the Inland Waterways Corporation. It was to become known to the public as the Federal Barge Line.

From the first moment the new enterprise was a success. Inspired by its example, other barge lines developed, privately owned lines now, with sleek new towboats. The people of the cities, rediscovering their river, again sent freight by water. And the balance between the Valley and the Coasts commenced to be restored. Old industries ceased moving away from the river towns, and new ones came to join them. The rebirth of the Valley had begun.

The towboat is accomplishing other results than the rebuilding of the Valley; it is adding a new and colorful life to the nation. The tow must be planned with the greatest precision. I know several towboat captains like Captain Alec who solve all their problems in advance with child's wooden blocks cut to the exact shape of their boats and barges. Each block bears the name and number of the vessel for which it is modeled; certain barges known as trouble makers because they are always breaking loose from their tows are marked with a distinguishing sign, like a red ribbon tied to the mane of a dangerous horse in a stable. It is a fascinating sight to watch Captain Alec toying with his blocks, constantly shifting their positions, just like a child on the morning after Christmas, with the important difference that these blocks represent several million dollars, and a slight mistake may mean disaster.

"Doggone, where'd I put that fuel flat," the sad-eyed Captain Alec will murmur to himself as he searches anxiously through the scarred wooden box which serves as his navy yard. "It's pretty near the finest block I've got and I'm always losing it. Somebody's been taking it, I'll bet, and practicing making up tows. I'm going to be mighty mad if they've lost my fuel flat."

He finds the missing vessel tucked away in a corner.

The actual making up of a tow is a difficult operation, much resembling the making up of a freight train. Captain Alec and his colleagues must weave their towboats in and out the barges with all the complications of an engineer in a switching yard preparing his train for California. And once formed, the tow is often shifted on the way. At times it must be three barges in width to give greater ease in steering through a swift current; at times the length is greatly increased to gain speed up slack water. But on occasions none of these devices avail, and the captain must resort to that most disliked of barge operations, double tripping. The tow is split in two; while one half is taken up the difficult stretch of river, the other is left moored to the bank in charge of a solitary deckhand, to await the towboat's return.

"There ain't nothing in towboating bad as double tripping," Slim, the watchman, said as he sat at the head of the boat, figuring with a piece of chalk on the deck the amount of pay he would have left when he reached St. Louis. "Looks like the captain always picks out the worst place on the river to tie up. Ain't never a town, with a pretty girl you could talk to or anything. It's always a big swamp, full of rattlesnakes, and moccasins. And the mosquitoes is so thick they're waving around like flags. You wrap yourself tight in a tarpaulin. But don't do no good. These mosquitoes is special double-tripping mosquitoes. When they can't get through the first trip, they make the trip twice. And when they've done eat you enough, one of 'em flies back to the water moccasins and says it's all right for them to come on now. And then you have moccasins climbing up your pants leg and going down your shirt. And when they get through, and the alligators stops a-hollering, you stretch out and think maybe you're going to get a little sleep. And just then a rowboat comes up quiet as a catfish, and half a dozen men climbs out and starts stealing the sugar in the barges to make moonshine. If you don't stop 'em the captain fires you, and if you stop 'em you get killed."

He looked mournfully at the result of his calculations on the deck. "I don't know. I'm a-going to quit the river, and give it back to the moccasins. How's this here iron working, putting up them big skyscrapers? That's pretty good work, ain't it? Anyways if you get killed, you get killed all at once, instead of dying slow on the river, like if you took poison."

The tows on the Mississippi are lashed with heavy ropes and metal lines, then tightened with huge ratchets until the ten or twelve barges become one vast barge floating like a long red island on the water. Suddenly the prows of the foremost barges will strike a sandbar developed overnight in the channel, or another great towboat sweeps past, its wheel churning the river into a tossing sea. The barges moan and screech in terror as they scrape each other's sides. Ratchets and lines snap explosively. In an instant the huge steel hulls go careening in all directions down the river, like a herd of panic-struck cattle fleeing before a storm. Frantically the towboat goes in pursuit, the captain blue with apoplexy and the mate roaring curses. After hours of frenzied labor, the vessels, wandered miles down the river, are collected one by one; the tow goes floundering on its troubled way.

The towboat has brought to the life of the river a human failing almost unknown in the days of the packet—homesickness. The packet was swift and its distances generally short. But the plodding towboat when it sets out on the journey between Pittsburgh and New Orleans must travel almost four thousand miles before it returns, a distance longer than the ocean voyage to Europe. It may be months before the departing crew once more see on the horizon the red glare of the steel mills that marks their homes. As a result, the towboat deckhands, particularly of the Pittsburgh lines, have developed a quality of resigned melancholy, much like the crew of a sailing ship. This melancholy grows as the Pittsburgher steams nearer and nearer to New Orleans, and only lessens when on the return journey he reaches Louisville and knows that he is "over the hill." Soon he will be back in the smoky metropolis; arrived there he can spend all his money in a few gay, fevered hours, and start on the long journey all over again.

The towboat deck hands form a distinct tribe in America, as individual as taxi drivers or policemen. At times they are callow youths still in their teens, at times they are old men with silvery beards. All are restless spirits, who go roving from boat to boat, cursing the river which gives them their life, leaving it at last for a job in a factory along the bank, only to return within three days because they heard a pretty steamboat whistle. Reckless, generous, spendthrift, they are always stranded on the riverman's beach without a penny; money exists for them only to be instantly spent. It is their boast that when the captains and pilots go to town, these mighty officers come walking back to the boat to save the carfare; the lowly deckhand arrives riding on the upholstered seat of a taxicab.

But theirs is indeed a hard life. They must hurry onto the ice-coated barges in a sleet storm, to twist icy lines and tighten ratchets when only a miracle prevents them from sliding into the water. They must wheel coal at night from the fuel flat, a task of constant danger, for they must work in inky blackness, as even a faint light would blind the pilot above. On such occasions their only aid is flour smeared along the edges of their wheelbarrows to make them shine a little in the blackness, and two other lines of flour brushed along the edges of the boards that form their perilous pathway over the water. Many a deckhand has gone down to a rivery grave with his wheelbarrow, because the night was foggy, and the flour lines did not shine clear.

Like all other river vessels, the towboats are rich in superstition. If a blackbird flies from the shore into the cook's galley, it is a certain sign that death has arrived or is on its way. It is very bad luck to row a yawl around the head of a vessel, or even to throw anything over the bow; and I know a captain who is reputed to discharge instantly anyone guilty of this breach of the river law. It is equal bad luck to bring aboard peanuts in the shell, because these will make the vessel go aground, though peanuts that are merely salted leave the craft quite unaffected. A bit of sassafras wood aboard is as deadly as the cobra to a human. And if the boat is at a landing with smoke drifting up from only one of its stacks, it would be well for the crew to order their coffins, as the vessel will sink before the trip is ended.

Just as there was racing in the olden days of the packet, so racing continues with its successors today. On the Ohio and the upper Mississippi locks and dams are frequent, and racing here has purpose as well as excitement. The first vessel to reach the lock is the first to pass through; with a long tow that must be split into numerous sections, losing first place may mean a delay of a number of hours, a serious matter when the captain is in a hurry to load a rush cargo, or the members of the crew are nearing their homes and waiting to spend their pay. Because of the numerous dams in the area, the Pittsburgh district is known as "the Pools," and there is one powerful towboat that wins these races with such consistency it is known to all its vanquished rivals as "The Bull of the Pools."

This racing breeds feuds, and the feuds breed more racing. There are bitter personal feuds between pilots of certain competing lines, and even between pilots employed by the same company. There are the feuds between those valiant upholders of the ancient tradition, the towboats that run by steam, and the "Deaf and Dumb" Diesel boats, those oily apostles of modernism. There are the feuds between the plodding towboats and the swift packets, the towboats grimly resenting the river code that forces them out of the entrance of a lock with their heavy burdens to let their graceful sisters pass.

The riverman has always been an animal lover, and wherever a towboat is found there is apt to be a pet on which he may lavish his affection.

"I seen all kinds of pets on towboats," drawled my friend Slim, the watchman, through a cocoanut cake he was munching. "I seen crows that could talk, and could get silver money away from you quicker than a pork chop butcher can get a dollar from a nigger on Saturday. Then the crow 'd hide it in a hole somewhere, and you'd never find it again. And I knowed a nanny goat named Juanita on a boat when I was decking, that was a terror. She had a big shaggy goat for a husband named Bill, and she led him a worse life that my wife 'd lead me, if I was ever home. Just bossed him all the time. She liked to roam around everywhere on the boat, and if a board going out to the barges didn't look like it was safe, she'd get Bill and make him walk over it first, and if he didn't fall in, then she knew it was all right. And then one day something happened. I don't know yet whether she done it on purpose, or was just feeling frisky. There was a big open place between the head of the boat and one of the barges. She looked at it a minute, like she was getting ready to jump, then decided to get Bill to try it for her, like he always done. He come over, and looked at the river between him and the tow, and you could see he was telling her it was too much for him to handle. She got awful mad and stamped her feet and hollered. Bill looked at the water again, and looked at Juanita screaming at him, and then he kind of shook all over, and jumped. He fell in the river and was drowned. Like I says, I don't know yet whether she done it on purpose. I don't trust women no-ways."

He chewed a new cake in reflection. "Yes sir, I seen all kinds of pets on towboats. I knowed a monkey slept on a leather belt fixed to some kind of machine down in the engine room. Just to have some fun with him, the engineer 'd try to catch him when he was sleeping and open the throttle easy so the belt 'd start moving and roll him on the floor. But no matter how quiet he walked, the monkey was always off the belt long before he ever got anywheres near that throttle. And after that to get even with the engineer, the monkey 'd take the oil can and hold it upside down and squeeze out every drop was in it, right in the middle of the floor, so the engineer 'd fall and break his neck maybe."

A giant deck hand, Red Pete, standing near by waved a huge paw to a girl on the shore. "Smartest animal I ever seen ain't on a towboat," he declared. "He's a dog they call Fats, stays on one of them Government locks up near Pittsburgh. Fats knows the whistle of every towboat comes there better than any pilot or deckhand on the river. All the towboats feeds him, peppermint candy, and crackerjack and things, and you can tell what boat's coming when the whistle blows just by watching Fats. He sleeps pretty near all the time, and if he gets all the way up and goes to the door and starts jumping around kind of excited, that's the *Steeltown Queen,* 'cause the fellows on her give him chocolate bars and vanilla wafers and everything. If he rolls over and gets up kind of slow but don't do no barking or jumping, that's the *Arthur Bartlett,* that gives him sandwiches and things, but nothing fancy like the other. But if he don't get up at all and just lays there like he was dead you can know that's the *Mollie Q.* 'Cause the captain of the *Mollie* don't like dogs, and they don't give him nothing. Yes sir. He's sure a smart dog, knows what he's doing. I decked on the *Mollie,* and they don't give the men nothing either."

The towboat lines are numerous today, and constantly increasing. The Federal Barge Line is now the largest river transportation system in the world. Three months would be

required for a round trip over its lines which extend from New Orleans to Minneapolis and St. Paul; up the muddy Missouri to Kansas City; in a grand loop around salt water to Mobile and the Warrior River; up the Illinois to Chicago and the strange-shaped cargo vessels of the Great Lakes.

But the other lines are large as well, and carry cargoes totalling many millions. There is the Union Barge Line of Pittsburgh, noted for its hospitality and its table, with some boats that are air-conditioned for the comfort of their crews; there is the Campbell Line of Pittsburgh, the American Barge Line of Louisville, and the Mississippi Valley Line of St. Louis, with its towboats that glide like ghostly mountains through the night; there are the lines of private industries, like the steel companies of Pittsburgh and the fleets of the oil company with the *Sprague,* the largest towboat in the river's history. So huge is this vessel, known affectionately as *Big Mama,* that she has become a contemporary legend like the mythical *Huronico,* flagship of Old Al. So powerful is the *Sprague's* wheel, says rumor, its waves disturb swimmers in the Bay of Rio de Janeiro; so lofty are her smokestacks she carries a twelve-inch water main slung between them to carry off the water from the clouds they are constantly scraping.

There are other smaller companies, like the old packets, where the river tradition survives in its least changed fashion. Among these is the Vicksburg and New Orleans Packet Company, whose valiant Captain Dick Dicharry, at a time when all the other packets in the lower river had vanished, continued to operate his famous *Tennessee Belle,* a twentieth-century Horatio at the Bridge, with only his courage and love of the river to aid him. His line, too, now carries so much freight it has been compelled to stop carrying passengers; the *Belle's* pet pig, Donaldsonville, grows so fat it refuses to rise even to be fed, and eats its supper lying on its side.

It is difficult for the land dweller when looking at a towboat to believe that these vessels are revolutionizing the interior of the nation. The towboat appears clumsy. It is always sticking on a sandbar. Often it moves upstream only half as fast as a man can walk. But the barges in which its nose is buried and which it shoves sturdily before it are in effect a great covered raft on which thousands of tons of freight may be piled; and the raft is one of the cheapest forms of transport known to man.

Men die, and factories crumble, and automobiles and railroad tracks and engines rust into the elements from which they were formed. But long after all traces of our troubled civilization have vanished, the Mississippi will still be rolling yellow to the sea.

And on it there will be some dweller of that distant time, with an oar or some curious wheel, who as he goes floating down toward the far world beyond the horizon, will push his belongings and those of his fellows on the logs linked before him, and will chant a song of praise to the God that created the waters, and gave them to men to be free.

The Lighter Side

VII

SHOWBOAT

THE theater is as old as man, and perhaps even older, dating to those shadowy times when only the animals roamed the earth. I have heard legends in far-off jungles of great monkeys who stood about a cleared space and danced in solemn rhythms while another monkey giant beat upon a hollow log that served as drum; I have heard legends of dogs who collected all their four-footed neighbors in a wide circle around them, and then proceeded to demonstrate the latest in canine headstands and flip-flops.

Long before the days of the historians, on a cold night in winter, some talented cave man undoubtedly sat before the fire entertaining his wife and his friends with imitations of the benighted cave men who lived on the opposite mountain; or he tossed three stones into the air, and keeping them constantly in motion before him, caught them now in his mouth, now in his ear or toes. With man's first written records, there appear the acrobats, the jugglers, the minstrels, the magicians, who roamed about the land gaining a few presents by a dance that imitated the movements of the great snakes lurking in the forests, or swallowed two swords where only one had ever been swallowed before. For always there have been those who work in the fields or the towns and those who entertain them when they have finished their labors; and so it will continue till the end of time. For the instinct of the actor is deep as life itself.

Probably in the earliest days of the Mississippi, when the Indians or the Mound Builders or their mysterious forerunners first traveled the waters of the great stream, some jovial individual sat in his hollowed log and sent it into a series of elaborate loops and dives for the benefit of all the other voyagers who might chance to be watching. Certain it is that with the first settlements of the white men along its shores, there were always some wanderers on a flatboat or a raft who would stop at a tavern on the bank, and for a few drinks of whisky and a bed, would sing a doleful ballad, accompanied by appropriate gestures, or exhibit a huge green parrot who could smoke a pipe or drink a swig of rum like a river pirate, and raucously clamor for more.

It was with such background and history that there arose

the picturesque floating theater of the Mississippi, the show-boat.

There is a twofold charm about a showboat. There is always glamor about the theater, with the gay, fevered life of its actors; there is always a fascination about a river with all the craft, great and small, that move ever down its waters. Despite a changing world where actors now emerge from curious electric bulbs or long strips of celluloid, the show-boat still survives, pursuing its vagrant way up and down the river, while the calliope blasts the air with its steamy tremolo, and children scramble down the banks to watch in awe and wonder.

It is an odd-looking structure, the typical showboat, re-sembling an old-time packet whose owner, in a fit of anger, has knocked off both the smokestacks and the pilot house; moored behind is a small steamboat, to move it on its jour-neyings. The vessel has changed little with the passing years. At one end is the stage, its wings piled high with scenes of ruined castles or a dusty, lamplit street corner of Old Chi-cago; the curtain depicts a bridge over some precipitous valley high in the Alps, or a horde of white-robed men and women fleeing terror-struck from the flames of Vesuvius in the Destruction of Pompeii. At the side of the curtain is a hole, through which the proprietor can peep unobserved and count the audience in the seats before him; when he has mentally translated the spectators into money that seems sufficient for the evening, he smiles with content and gives the orchestra the signal to begin.

There are five large showboats on the inland rivers today: the *Goldenrod* and the *Hollywood*, with their headquarters at St. Louis, owned by Captain Billy Menke and his brothers, who have long been a noted theatrical family on the river;

Bryant's Showboat that plies between Cincinnati and Point Pleasant in West Virginia, with its colorful Captain Billy Bryant, pitchman, showman, author, who will steer a boat or adapt Hamlet with equal facility; the *Majestic* which glides up the northern reaches of the winding Ohio, and the mountain bordered Allegheny and Monongahela; and the new *Dixie Queen,* just out from Kansas City on the muddy Missouri, lazily drifting eastward or wherever her fancy wills. There are other, smaller boats, unknown to the world of the theater, which the traveler may encounter far up some distant tributary; woebegone craft, with a few rusty iron tables set out for drinks and sandwiches, and a tiny stage where a wan-eyed girl sings a melancholy song of the hills and a young man in a suit of threadbare green plays the guitar in doleful accompaniment.

"Guess I've seen some pretty funny times," said the genial Captain Billy Menke, as we sat on the deck of the *Goldenrod* at St. Louis, and watched a towboat pushing some oil-barges up the water. "But I guess about the funniest was one night up near Pittsburgh. It was February, bitter cold, and we were just starting to go South for the season. We backed out from the wharf, when all of a sudden there was a bump, and the boat began acting mighty queer. I ran down in the hold, and I heard a terrible gurgling, and when I got my flashlight going, I saw a hole as big as a man's body right in her prow where she'd hit a piling. She was starting to sink, and I knew if I didn't do something mighty quick, in about two seconds she'd be at the bottom of the river. And then I had an idea. Maybe it was the story I read when I was in school about the Dutch boy that put his finger in the dike and saved the city. Anyway, I jumped right square into the break where the water was coming through, to plug it with my body.

It was a big hole, but I was a pretty husky fellow in those days. I went through as far as my stomach, and stopped. I couldn't squeeze down any further."

Captain Billy lit one of the heavy black cigars beloved of rivermen, and smoked it cheerfully. "Well, I stayed in that water I don't know how many hours, while they tried to swing her around and beach her. It was bitter cold, and my brothers and the crew kept bringing whisky to keep me warm. I'm not much of a drinker, but I sure took it that night. It was daylight when they got her landed. But I was happy. Not a teaspoonful of water had got past me. And my brothers said I plugged that hole so tight, when they pulled me out I popped, just like the cork in a bottle of champagne."

The plays on the larger boats are either melodrama or musical spectacles, the melodramas being acted in burlesque fashion when the boat is anchored at the wharf of a metropolis, but losing all such artificial quality the moment the vessel points its prow toward the wilderness. Always their programs are broken with vaudeville: a Swiss bell ringer; a musician who can play Dixie on the flute as he swings from a horizontal bar; an artist who can draw a picture of the President in red, white, and blue chalk upside down, and balance a huge American flag on his right shoe during the entire creation of the masterpiece.

These talented vaudevillians are performers in the main drama as well. For an actor on a showboat is nothing if not versatile. He must play the cornet in the orchestra for the overture before the rise of the curtain; when the drama begins he must portray the bearded father giving advice to his fair young daughter about to set off on her perilous journey to the city. He must sell popcorn and ice cream

cones during the first intermission and stop to play an ac-
cordion solo; when the play begins again, he must enact
the hind-end of a horse and the woodcutter that flags the
train bearing the hero and his love to their destruction. He
must do a tap dance; play the piano strings with a nail as
though it were a harp; ride roller skates on a barrel; and one
minute before the final curtain be thrown to his death to the
Indians waiting in triumph at the foot of Grand Canyon.

The actors on the showboats are of infinite variety. Some
are carnival troupers, dancers and acrobats, come from the
tents of the sideshows; some are country boys and girls, lured
by the glamor of the theater from the cornfields and the
pastures of their fathers; some are professional actors, like
those in the old stock companies, weary of trouping in one
night stands and the vagaries of the metropolis. The smaller
boats are family affairs, a man and his wife, with any roving
performer they may chance upon in their travels, who for a
night or two will enchant the rural spectators as he covers
a rubber comb with a piece of paper and imitates a train
climbing a hill, or presents a dog that with considerable
assistance plays three bars of Swanee River on a cheap banjo.

The career of the showboater is unpredictable, filled with
the uncertainty that has always been the lot of the actor,
suddenly lifting him from poverty to riches, then plunging
him back to starvation more desperate than before.

"It's a great life, if you can live through it," said Captain
Billy as we took seats on the stage where the actors were
gathering for a rehearsal of next week's performance. "The
worst part's getting started. I won't forget my first trip in a
hurry. There were four of us brothers, and we'd always
wanted a showboat, so we scraped up every cent we could
and bought us a little one. We decided we'd take her on the

upper Mississippi. It was cold weather, and all the steamboatmen told us we'd sure get in trouble going North that
way. But we were kids, and we knew better. We hadn't been
out three days, when the coldest winter in thirty-five years
hit the river. It froze solid, and we were right in the middle,
like the girl in the ice cake you've seen, I guess, only she
gets paid for it. We couldn't move an inch. We stayed there
a week, and the ice didn't break, and then two weeks, and
then three weeks, and things got pretty bad. Every penny we
had was gone, and in no time all the canned food we'd
brought with us was used up, too. And then we began going
hungry. Only thing we had left on the boat was some rolled
oats, and after about a week of it, taking the oats was worse
than not eating. Plenty of times we swore we'd die before we
swallowed another spoonful. We'd go without it a whole day
and crawl in bed and go to sleep hoping we wouldn't come
out till we were dead, and then we'd wake up with a lot of
banging around the kitchen at two or three in the morning.
And we'd know somebody had gotten too hungry and was
cooking rolled oats again. So we'd all get up, and eat with
him, then curse and crawl back in bed."

A whistle blew hoarsely in the distance. Captain Billy listened in thought. "I guess the cold was even worse than the
oats. The engineer used to say if you'd stand on deck and
blow a good breath, it'd turn into an icicle and fall down
and break your toe. All the coal was gone for the stove in
the cabin, and the thermometer kept dropping lower and
lower. We just sat around by that icy stove, shivering. I
guess they'd have found us dead some morning, frozen stiff,
if one day we hadn't happened to see a man on shore getting
rid of a lot of old automobile tires, and the engineer said
rubber 'd burn. So we went over and got 'em. They'd burn

all right, when you started 'em with scraps of wood and news-paper, but the smell of that rubber was so bad it pretty nearly killed us. The engineer said for ten years after he couldn't stand rubber anywhere around him. He'd take every rubber out of his pencils and even pull the rubber threads from his suspenders. He said once somebody just bounced a rubber ball near him when he was standing in front of a store, and he started shivering so hard he broke a plate glass window."

The advance agent and the billposter are an important part of the showboat crew. For days ahead, they travel before the vessel, plastering up their gaudy announcements on fences and buildings or putting a card in the window of a drowsy grocery. Adventures befall them constantly. A bill-poster I know was traveling in a rattletrap car through a little river valley noted for the violence of its residents, and had made ready to fix a flamboyant lithograph on a barn wall, when to his horror, as the brush went up for the first stroke, a bullet went squarely through the bristles. Three times he lifted the brush above his head; three times a bullet sang past him. At last, certain he had in some way offended the wild natives, he snatched up brushes, bills, and pastepots, and made a frantic dash for his car. He was clambering hastily inside, when a lanky mountaineer came out from the bushes where he had been hiding.

"Don't stop, brother," the newcomer pleaded. "I ain't a-meaning you no harm. Carnival's a-coming in about a month with a shooting gallery gives you a five dollar bill if you can hit six of them tin ducks a-moving. I didn't get the money last year but I done made up my mind this time I'm sure going to win her. That there brush the way she goes up and down's the jumpingest thing I ever seen next to them

ducks. I practices thataway with a billposter every time I kin."

In a similar isolated section, inhabited by moonshiners who had balked every visit of the Federal officers, there is a legend of two clever Federal men who determined they would end this whisky making forever. Waiting until the season when the showboats were expected, they disguised themselves as billposters, and hiring a horse and wagon, drove along the river road, pasting up their bright colored streamers, and calling an amiable salutation to every passer-by. For several days their work went on without incident, and their spirits grew gay. They were certain that they were unsuspected. The showboatmen were the friends of every traveler on the highway; soon the officers would know the location of the most remote still in the valley. Late one morning they stopped for lunch in the square of a little river town crowded with towering figures whose clothing reeked with the telltale odor of corn mash. Three boys sat on the broken curbstone, drowsily gazing at the green hills beyond the water.

One of the officers put a quarter in the hand of the eldest of the trio, a gaunt-faced youth wearing shabby overalls. "Keep an eye on the horse and wagon, will you, boys?" he asked. "We're going down to the restaurant to get us something to eat."

The gaunt-faced youth tucked the coin into his pocket, and let his eyes drift off lazily to the horizon once more. He spoke at last, gravely. "What you want us to do with the horse and wagon after you don't come back?" he asked.

The revenue men gazed at him in shocked silence. A moment later, they shook their heads mournfully, and emptying the paste buckets into the gutter, turned their wagon in the dusty roadway, and slowly drove back to the lowlands from which they had come.

The relations between the showboats today are of extreme cordiality. But only a few years ago competition was unmerciful. An advance man would come to a region a few days after the visit of a rival, and carefully cover up the banners of his predecessor with his own gaudy lithographs. Captains constantly tried to deceive each other about their schedules, so that they might be the first to arrive on some profitable river. For the first boat of the new season because of its novelty was certain to attract crowds that strained the doors.

Two rival owners, with their boats laid up for the winter, would chance to meet at supper in the dining room of some little river-town hotel. The fat Northerner, Captain Sandy, owner of the showboat *Morning Star,* would look thoughtfully across the table at Captain Ollie, the white moustached Southerner who was proprietor of the showboat, *Golden Princess.*

"When you starting out this year, Captain Ollie?" the owner of the *Morning Star* would ask, as the waitress brought two dishes of rice pudding and set them on the red cloth.

Captain Ollie would watch the quiet-spoken owner of the *Golden Princess.* Making a tunnel through the mound of rice pudding with his spoon, he would chew a moment in reflection. "Looks like I ain't going to get started till mighty late this year, Captain Sandy. Got a terrible lot of repairs to do. Stage has got to be all fixed up, and have to put on a whole new roof, and maybe put all new seats in her. Don't see any way I can get started before the first of June."

The fat Captain Sandy would nod in sympathy. Tasting

the pudding, he would bury it under a thick shroud of sugar. His round countenance would grow long with melancholy. "Looks like I'm worse off than you, Captain Ollie. Steamboat inspectors been after me bad. Got to buy a whole new set of boilers, and I can't even get 'em delivered till the middle of July. And I got to put a new wheel on her, and change all the steering gear. I can't get started till the first of August, anyway. Looks to me I'll be lucky this year if I get a month on the river."

Captain Ollie would enlarge the tunnel in the pudding, and fill it with some peach preserves from a glass jar on the table. "You ain't going up the Ohio this year, are you, Captain Sandy? I've sure made my last trip on the Ohio, myself. She used to be a mighty good showboat river. But those country towns on her are all played out now. I wouldn't go near 'em with a trained flea show."

Captain Sandy would nod in emphatic assent. "You sure won't catch me going up there any more, Captain Ollie. Ohio's all right for a shantyman, maybe. But for a showboater it's just good to wash his clothes."

A month later, on the first day of February, in the midst of a howling blizzard, the fat Captain Sandy would cast off his lines, and head for the hill-girded Ohio. And as he reached Cairo and swept into the mouth of the yellow stream, even from the distance he could see some gay colored pictures tacked upon the fences along the river road. They were the bills of a showboat. Captain Ollie had been there a week before.

In addition to the billposters and the advance men, there are numerous means by which the showboat may lure its customers. One captain I know occasionally hires a hearse, with a flower-decked coffin resting conspicuously within; behind it trails the cast, garbed in funeral costumes, and weeping copiously as they carry a banner: "He died laughing at the showboat." Another captain, friendly with the telephone operator of a minute hamlet, brings the showboat band to the dwelling which serves as the telephone exchange, and after the operator has rung the bells of the farmers for a radius of many miles so that they are all ready with receivers at their ears, proceeds to direct the musicians in a half-hour concert of the best in their repertoire. There is also the method of the parade, almost vanished now, because of city laws passed by dull councilmen. And last, and most important, there is the calliope.

There are perhaps few persons in America who have not at some time in their lives heard the strange steamy sobbing of the circus calliope as it rolls on its sonorous way before the red-painted cages of the rhinoceros and the zebras in a picturesque procession of the Greatest Show on Earth. But it is only those fortunate dwellers on the river banks who have heard the calliope of a showboat, beside which the voice of the circus calliope becomes like the cry of a new-born kitten when compared to the roar of a lion.

It is a difficult art, the playing of the showboat calliope. The musician who is monarch of these hissing keys is generally the pianist in the stage orchestra, and perhaps Othello or Raffles in the evening's drama as well; so deafening is the noise of the instrument, his ears are often stuffed with cotton, in order that his hearing may last for tomorrow. Not only does the art require musical knowledge; it demands a quick wit and ingenuity as well. For on most showboat calliopes, keys are always missing or refusing to move under the pressure of a finger; the player must improvise some instant transition to bridge the void in the melody, a fact which explains those sudden dolorous sighs with which every devotee of the calliope is so familiar. Of all the songs that thunder over the housetops of the river towns, Old Kentucky Home is the favorite. Strangely, no such reverence is accorded Home Sweet Home on a certain vessel of my acquaintance, for its playing is deemed as dangerous as the lighting of a match in a gas-filled coal mine. Once a visiting lady musician was rendering this famous composition on the calliope, when the showboat, with no apparent reason except the power of suggestion, considerably embarrassed the player and the crew by deciding to seek its home in the bottom of the river.

For hundreds of years misguided individuals regarded all actors as outcasts, members of a class so degraded they could not even be buried in a country churchyard. In certain distant towns on the river, this opinion still prevails today. And in such communities the life of the showboat captain is doubly full of trial. He must pay a license fee so high, it often prevents the vessel from even landing at the wharf; a rigid ordinance forbids the passing of handbills or the playing of the calliope anywhere within the county. Equally difficult are the towns where law is lacking, those centers of lumbering and mining and steel-making which have lost little of the robustness marking their origin. Particularly on Saturday night, the showboat captain, in such lusty areas, keeps steam at full pressure in the boilers, ready to take to flight up the river when the exuberance of his visitors approaches the point of riot and revolution.

"Sure had a fine time a couple of years ago," said Doc, the red-headed fireman on a showboat, as we sat in a wagon diner near the waterfront eating doughnuts and coffee. "Captain's always figuring up something new, and this here season

I'm telling you about, he fixed him up a baseball game. A team from the boat 'd go ashore and play a team in the town, and all the town people 'd get to talking about it and we done mighty good business. Course we always let them people in the town win, 'cause we knowed if we didn't they'd get mad and stay away from the show. Wasn't easy to lose all the time, though, 'cause we had a new actor was the leading man, a young fellow had been some kind of fancy player on a college ball team or something, and he was mighty proud of the way he could play. Captain told him if he wanted to get back home alive, he'd better forget he ever knowed anything. He done all right, till we come to a town was the toughest place on the river. It was a mining and lumber town both, and there wasn't a man in her didn't pack a gun. The barber there told me they was so tough the kids begun shaving when they was two, and the teachers wouldn't let 'em start to school until they'd killed three men. Well, the team from the boat went on the bank to play the town, like they always done. But I don't know, something was sure wrong that day, 'cause whatever we done, looked like we just couldn't keep from winning. Pretty soon the bases was full, and the crowd begun grumbling, and I could see they was getting mighty ugly. It was the young college fellow's turn at bat, so the captain goes up to him.

" 'For God's sake, strike out, Joe,' he says. 'If you don't our leg bones is going to be souvenir canes these kids 'll hang on the trees here next Christmas.'

"The fellow nods his head he understands. And then he made two strikes, and I figured he was all right. Then the third ball come over, and he swung at it to miss, and he knocked a home run must have landed in Canada. In about a second the place was full of men running, and they wasn't running on bases neither. They was big fellows, all carrying clubs and guns, and yelling and hollering like they was crazy. We run for the boat and tried to get her out in the water. But it was too late. All them fellows come aboard. And when they got through—I ain't lying when I tell you—they'd chopped that boat up so fine there wasn't a chip of wood on her long enough for you to play jackstraws, and there wasn't a piece of window glass big enough to set for a diamond chip in a ten cent store ring."

The showboat captain must be ever ready to meet the new and the unexpected, and so develops a resourcefulness often absent in the rest of humankind. He must know how to argue with a grafting politician who threatens to close the show if a huge bribe is not produced by noon of the next day. He must know, when an actor suddenly quits him just before the rising of the curtain, how to rearrange the part so that a telephone is introduced into the play, and at the proper intervals, all the lines of the missing tragedian are read over the telephone wire by some actor hidden in the wings. He must know how to keep his actors and his crew from starving when the land is seared by drought. He must know, when all other expedients fail, how temporarily to abandon show-boating, and transform his vessel into a freight boat, with the stage full of bundles of brooms and rolls of carpet, and the seats occupied by sacks of potatoes, like dull-witted humans refusing to applaud.

I am acquainted with the captain of a showboat, who once, when his business had reached the point of extinction, happened to land at a settlement where the ferry that ran to the opposite shore had broken its wheel, leaving the inhabitants helpless to cross the river. Quickly the captain decided to become a ferryman. Day and night he sent his awkward craft lumbering across the water, with a negro stationed on each bank holding a great cowhorn to summon him over whenever there were paying passengers. At last the broken wheel of the regular ferry was repaired and it made ready to resume its old duties; the showboat captain turned the nose of his vessel down the river and went joyfully on his way, his pockets filled with money to start a new triumphal tour.

But perhaps one of the oddest emergencies ever confronting a showboat owner was that which arose on a vessel where Doc was the fireman. "We was playing in a little town in Arkansas," Doc related, as he waved his skinny hand amiably to a fellow riverman coming through the door of the wagon diner, where we still sat talking over our coffee. "There was a lot of bank robberies going on was being done by a fellow they called Kitten Face, had broke out of jail and was killing everybody come near him, and one night the captain was working the lights for the first act when the cook come up and said somebody wanted to see him. He went outside, and it was the sheriff.

" 'Take it easy, Captain,' the sheriff says. 'I got something to tell you is going to give you a shock. Kitten Face is in there watching the show. I'm down here all by myself and you and all your boys got to help me catch him. He's sitting on the end seat in the third row. There's a ten thousand dollar reward out for him. If we catch him, I'll split the reward.'

"Well, the Captain didn't feel so good, I guess. 'Cause he didn't have a gun that'd work anywhere on the boat. But he was a pretty smart fellow. He was playing a big musical show, with a lot of Chinese soldiers and knights in tin armor, and American marines, and things. So he got all the prop battle axes, and the tin swords for the Chinamen, and the wooden guns for the marines, and when the intermission come, he told us what he was going to do. We looked through the peephole in the curtain and we could see Kitten Face sitting there, sort of sulking, until one of the show girls come along selling popcorn, and he brightened up, and bought a package from her, and begun eating it. A couple of minutes after, the curtain went up for the second act. This act was where one of the marines sees a Chinese girl in a garden that he gets into by mistake—it was a awful funny show. And he's starting to make love to her, when all of a sudden the stage and the whole theater goes black. Then the lights goes on again. And all around where Kitten Face is sitting there's a lot of Chinese soldiers holding tin swords and battleaxes that bend when they hit you and U. S. Marines pointing wooden guns that wouldn't shoot a split pea. Right in the middle of 'em was the sheriff with his pistol.

" 'We got you, Kitten,' he grumbled. 'Won't do you no good trying to fight.'

"Well, this Kitten Face was a whopper, six feet four, and a dead shot with his gun, and whenever they tried to catch him before, they'd always send fifty or a hundred men in the swamps to get him. He could have took that sheriff and cracked him between his little finger and his thumb, just like one of them soft-shell walnuts. But he looked around at them marines and the Chinamen, and he went all white.

" 'I know when I ain't got a chance,' he said. 'Put on the handcuffs, sheriff.'

"And he went off that showboat like a baby lamb following its mother in a Oklahoma tornado.

"Captain never got the reward money, though. I guess they didn't want to chalk up no more murders against Kitten Face. 'Cause they knowed if a showboat captain ever got five thousand dollars all at once, he'd die in his tracks quicker than if he'd been hit over the heart by a whip snake."

It is a rich life, the life of the showboater. Hour after hour I have sat on the deck and watched the colorful pageant that moves up and down its creaking gangplank. The blonde-haired, stage-struck girl run away from her husband, pleading tearfully for the part of the ingénue; the grizzled fisherman shambling up from his rowboat to trade a huge catfish for a pound of sugar and a ticket to the show; the bearded captain of a towboat moored alongside come in to lament the low stage of the water; two swarthy men and a girl sauntered over from a neighboring carnival to say that their triple ladder act, the Mile High Indians, will rouse the coldest showboat audience from its apathy and bring it to its feet with clamorous cheers.

And it is a heroic life. The young leading man of the play, engaged in a tightrope act during an intermission, may fall and break his leg, for tightrope walking is doubly difficult on a showboat, due to the swaying of the vessel in the wake of a passing tow; instead of taking to his bed, as would most land dwellers, he dons a wig, and with his injured limb in splints, abandons all his youthful roles to enact the part of a crippled old man. I know a showboat woman who each evening hung by her teeth from a rubber mouthpiece fixed to a wire overhead, and while the orchestra played the Blue Danube, swung high over the heads of the enthralled audience. One night her grip failed, and while the audience cried out in horror, she dropped like a stone to the floor. For months she lay in bed, helpless, suffering, while the doctors informed her that besides the graver injuries, her teeth had all been loosened in their sockets. They forbade her to ever again swing from the circling wire. She made no answer.

But one morning, while no one was watching, she arose from her bed, and found the rubber mouthpiece in the bureau where it had lain since the night of the accident. Suspending it from a cord tied to a hook in the wall, she set the rubber in her mouth, and started practicing her old profession. Each day, with excruciating pain, she continued, now putting her weight on one tooth, now on another, with the time gradually growing longer and longer; until at last will had triumphed over physical weakness, and she went back to her gay whirling over the heads of the spectators in loops more dextrous and breath-taking than before.

As in the plays on the bare-walled stages, during a few crowded hours the showboat actors may run the gamut of human emotions, from ecstasy to despair. Trapped in a flood that each instant threatens to destroy them, or tortured by the mosquitoes of the Gulf drifting like streamers of fog over the boat, most of them know full well that their names will never be written in the glaring lights of far-off Broadway. Most of them know that like all true artists, whether they be actors, painters, writers, musicians, it is in their work that they must find their reward, for only the poorhouse awaits them in the end. Yet they are among the happiest of the earth's wanderers.

For besides the spell of the player, from which no human once touched by its mysterious power ever escapes, they are enthralled by another spell that is older than time, the magic of running water.

I do not know which spell is the stronger. I do not believe there is any showboater who can truly say. But most mortals are deemed fortunate if they possess a single love; the showboatman is doubly blessed, for he is permitted two.

VIII

MAGIC IN THE WILLOWS

THERE must be some curious property in the atmosphere lying over the Mississippi which causes all the craft floating upon its muddy surface to acquire a rich mellowness.

This quality is evident in every steamboatman as well, whether he be a member of the crew of a huge towboat pushing a million-dollar cargo of steel and automobiles, or of some minute vessel escorting a single barge of coal.

As part of this mellowness and genial appreciation of life in all its phases, every riverman is a born storyteller. Particularly the art flourishes aboard a packet boat, with its passengers who provide a perfect audience for the imaginative inventions of the crew. Here as the boat sails silently beneath the clouds, arise the legends of the river, like the fairy tales of the Irish and the ghost stories of the Scots; here are born the legends of that greatest steamboat of all time, the giant *Hurinoco,* so tall the eagles were always nesting in the smokestacks and spoiling the drafts, and which possessed a wheel so huge its driving shafts went into the cylinder heads today and came out tomorrow.

Every pilot, every roustabout, of the packet *Golden Eagle* at St. Louis can recount some vivid fact or fable, typically American. From Captain Buck, the vessel's master, the voyager may hear the true story of Captain Jack and the famous prophecy.

"We've had some pretty wonderful weather prophets on the river," Captain Buck declared to me amiably, as he chewed the end of his black cigar. "But the best of 'em all, I guess, was Captain Jack, who owned some steamboats up one of the tributaries. Every riverman in the Valley figured he was safe as a church as long as Captain Jack was around, because they figured nothing was going to happen up where they make the weather without Captain Jack's knowing about it days and weeks before. And then one day he met a pretty girl on shore and he fell in love and decided to get married. He went off with his bride for a long honeymoon. The rivermen were feeling pretty low. They'd been counting on Captain Jack for their weather reports as long as they could remember. Now every time they looked up at the sky, they were scared to death; they couldn't figure out whether it was going to be a clear day or a tornado.

"Then one morning in June, right in the middle of some beautiful weather, without a streak of cloud anywhere, one of the wharfmasters got a telegram. 'For God's sake, rush all your crews aboard, and get your hatches fastened down, and tie up your barges with every line you can steal or borrow.'

"The telegram was from Captain Jack, way out in San Francisco.

"The wharfmaster sent the news up and down the river as fast as he could, and all the pilots looked at the beautiful blue sky and wondered. But they did what Captain Jack said. The next day the worst cyclone that ever hit the river rolled all the way from St. Paul to New Orleans. It's a fine thing to be able to tell the weather like that all the way from California."

Even the rats on a packet boat acquire special and remarkable habits. The packet-boat rat lives far down in the darkness of the hold, known only to an occasional adventurous roustabout; in the black river silences he studies the rules of navigation with all the intentness of a cub pilot applying for a license. One of his first accomplishments is to learn the difference between the signals for a way landing and a regular landing, the way landing being one of those hasty pauses when the boat merely thrusts her nose against the bank an instant to let the roustabouts throw off a few bags of sugar to some waiting moonshiners. The veteran packet-boat rat has acquired the philosophic calm of the river, and when the bell rings for one of these hurried debarkments, he evinces no interest. Should the signal, however, be for a long stay, his ears become taut and his entire demeanor changes. Excitedly he prepares to go ashore. The instant the gangplank falls, he dashes ahead of the passengers and the crew, and gaily hurries off to visit his friends and sweethearts in the most comfortable cellars and attics of the town.

There he remains, nibbling the delicacies his hosts have provided, and exchanging the gossip of the river for the

gossip of the land, until the whistle blows, when he comes scrambling down the levee, leaping aboard just as the boat is pulling out from the dock. Only the young, unsophisticated rat, nervous from inexperience, will come on the vessel at the ring of the warning bell half an hour before the departure.

Occasionally tragedy befalls and a rat is left behind. Unhappily the careless one passes the hours and days until the vessel returns; some time after the boat has landed, he comes shambling onto the deck, trying to appear casual and indifferent before the taunts of his laughing fellows.

The roustabouts of the *Golden Eagle* are rich in information that embraces all branches of human activity. From them the traveler may learn how if he has a child that is crippled in the legs, to cure it he has only to let it walk in a wet sand pile; he must then carefully pick up the tracks and throw them over the roof of his house, and the child will soon be on its way to recovery.

If the traveler has an illness that is causing a high temperature, let him put an ax under the bed where he is sleeping, with the blade turned upward; it will cut the fever without fail.

And this information may be of the importance of life or death when it involves an enemy who has planted lizard or snake dust and caused the reptile to grow again inside his victim's body.

"I had a brother, Iron Man, they called him, worked on the old *Harry Lee*," said High Wire, a lofty negro with a scar running the entire length of his forehead, as we sat on the *Eagle* watching the Missouri shore drift past. "A woman what didn't like him planted a snake inside him. And it growed and growed in his stomach till he had to buy ten pounds of steak every day to keep it going. 'Cause if he didn't keep it fed, it'd bite his sides till he'd jest be dancing. And

then one day a girl he was a-going with told him what to do. First he got a sponge and tied it to a string. And then he dipped the sponge in some nice fresh milk, and he swallowed it. Snakes is crazy about milk, and he kept a-moving the sponge up and down in his stomach, and pretty soon the snake grabbed it. Iron Man jerked the sponge out mighty quick, and the snake come with it. He sure got rid of that snake. And he got something mighty fine, too. 'Cause a fellow from a circus come and bought the snake from him for four dollars."

"But I reckon what's worse than planting something inside you is woman trouble," continued High Wire after some reflection. " 'Cause when you got woman trouble, you got all the trouble there is. If you're done married to a woman and you want to git away, look around when she's sleeping, and you can find where she's got you all tied up in kind of knots somewheres, in a piece of string or thread or something. It's worst if it's blue string. You take a scissors and cut it, and you can git away any time. If you want a girl to marry you and she won't pay no attention, draw her name what they calls zigzag on a piece of paper, and swallow it. That night she'll come knocking at the door, and ask you to go off to the preacher."

The *Gordon C. Greene* of Cincinnati is another packet rich in river lore. Over a glass of the Vichy constantly before him, Captain Tom, the vessel's master, quietly talked of his famous mate Bill Cropper. "Bill was sure a great one," he declared. "Nothing ever came up, storm, flood, or general destruction that Bill wasn't ready to meet it head on. Once up near Marietta, Ohio, the boat got stuck on a sandbar. We tried everything to work her off, walking sticks to jump her, hoses to wash out the mud, everything a riverman ever heard of. But nothing did a bit of good and it looked like we were going to have to be stuck there till next high water. But then Bill got mad, and when Bill got mad things happened. The lower deck was loaded with turkeys we were taking to market. Bill took all the turkeys out of their coops, and got the carpenter to fasten staples over their feet. A couple of minutes later he ordered the rousters to take stations around the deck, and gave them all towels and aprons and any kind of rag he could lay his hands on. Then he blew a whistle and the rousters all started waving the cloths over their heads and yelling 'Shoo! Shoo!' And the turkeys flew up and lifted the boat right over into deep water. Bill was always a great help to a steamboat."

Captain Tom stopped a moment to order another glass of Vichy. "And then there's the story about Bill and the dice. I can swear to this one on a barge load of Bibles. My father was a little old-fashioned and didn't like gambling, and one day when there'd been a little trouble among the negroes over a crap game, he issued an order there'd be no more crap shooting allowed on the boat. This was just about too much for the roustabouts, and they all walked off. Father cancelled the order, but it was too late. We couldn't get them back with anything, and the boat couldn't sail without its crew. So Bill Cropper did some quick thinking again. He got himself the biggest pair of dice he could find—they were big as suitcases, the way I remember—and then went to the head of the boat and began to roll 'em with as much noise as he could, playing all by himself, and talking to the dice like they were his children. The rousters on shore moved closer and closer to the boat to watch. Bill didn't pay any attention to 'em, just kept playing. In a few minutes they were coming on the boat one at a time, and standing in a circle all around him. Pretty soon he slipped away somehow. But the dice went on rolling."

On a dark, moonless night, when the boat steams eerily up the black water, Captain Tom may be induced to tell the *Greene* superstitions; how it is very bad luck to have a round pilot house instead of a square one, and how the line has spent thousands of dollars altering the shapes of pilot houses when it chanced to purchase one that was circular. He will explain how it is very bad luck to have a steamboat with the letter M—the thirteenth letter—as an initial, which is why the line has never named a boat for his mother, the famous Captain Mary. He will quietly recount the recent craft whose names begin with M and which have suffered disaster: the *Morro Castle,* the *Macon.* And the Greene Line, which like the other packet lines of today, has never lost a passenger, is taking no chances.

The roustabouts on the *Gordon Greene* have the same magical learning as their fellows of the West and the South. I was talking to Big Un, a huge roustabout that handled the lines, and our talk drifted to ventriloquism. "It's mighty fine, that there voice throwing," Big Un said, as he moved his great legs an inch to allow another rouster to go to sleep on the rough boards beside him. "It's mighty fine if you can learn it. You can git money out of the air, and you git power over everybody comes near you, if you throws it jest right. But if you can't git it back after you done throwed it away, you sure better look out. I had a friend, Alligator they called him, lived in Covington, 'cross the river in Kentucky, that started to fool with this here voice throwing. First he throwed it far as the wall of the room, and then he throwed it across the street, and then he started to getting smart and throwing it down to Lexington and Paducah. And before he knowed it a hoodoo woman in Paducah took a hold of it and wouldn't let it go. For a couple of weeks he couldn't say nothing, jest went around working his mouth and making funny signs with his hands. And then one afternoon he was a-standing down by the river when the hoodoo woman throwed his voice back to him, all at once. It was jest like a big fish net, the people said that seen it, and it came so fast it jest choked him to death. Them big doctors come from the City Hall in Covington and looked at him a minute and took him away to bury him. And they said his face had all swelled up jest like he was hung. No sir, I don't want no fooling with that voice throwing."

The *Tennessee Belle* of New Orleans is another limitless mine of colorful fact and picturesque legend. The voyager

The Gordon C. Greene

can learn from Captain Dick's negroes all about the habits of the wily raccoon, who, when he wishes some honey, merely studies the directions in which two bees are flying, and watching where the lines of their flight cross each other, with the accuracy of a surveyor calculates the exact location of the hive. When this reconnaissance has been completed, the coon rolls himself again and again in a mud bank until he is completely encased by a clay armor; soon after he goes on his cautious way to raid the treasure trove. The traveler can learn how the panther, off in the cypress swamps beyond the levee, is one of the world's best ventriloquists, and by putting its paw in front of its mouth just before issuing its blood-curdling cry, is able to throw its voice so that the deer or human it is pursuing cannot tell in what direction the danger lies, and falls an easy victim. And there are the legends of the famous goats of the Anchor Line, those white, immaculate wanderers who were the sacred Indian bulls of the river. Regally these goats consented to stay aboard a boat of the line as long as they were treated in kingly fashion; when they felt their majesty slighted or wanderlust overcame them, they would hurry ashore and wait solemnly at the wharf until another Anchor vessel came around the bend. But never, in all their wanderings, and all their changes, did they make a mistake and set a hoof aboard the vessel of a competitor.

There is much to learn from the shantymen who come to the *Belle* with their catfish and game to brighten the steamboat table. An old shantyman on the *Belle's* route has a little fish dock where he sells his catch to the people of the near-by towns. No matter how often he changes his location, and no matter how difficult the maneuvering in a swift current, he always anchors the boat so that its door is facing upstream.

"Do it so she'll catch good luck," he declares. "You can catch good luck with an open door just the same as fish in a net. And the way to catch it is facing upstream, 'cause the good luck comes down the river, she never goes up. If you put the door facing any other ways, you might as well get yourself laid out in your coffin."

Every packet-boat whistle has its legends. Steamboat whistles are the diamonds, the platinum of the river. Lives have often been risked to rescue a whistle lost on some unlucky vessel foundered in a treacherous eddy. Peculiarly valued are the whistles of many tones, with pipes like those of an organ, and special whistles like that of the old *Natchez*, named for the Natchez Indians, and which carried a whistle that blew an Indian war whoop.

The whistle on the *Tennessee Belle* is one of the most beautiful on the river, rich and deep like a bass singer of the opera. The roustabout judges the pilot, not by his skill in steering the boat through the shoals and eddies of the river, but by the length of time he blows the whistle. "It's thisaway about them pilots," declares Uncle Jesse, the withered old negro who serves sometimes as roustabout and sometimes as cabin boy on the vessel. "If a pilot blows a whistle so long it gits the boat to shaking and knocks down the saucers on the shelves in the cookhouse, that there's a mighty fine pilot. That there's a man 'll never git you into no kind of trouble. But if he's one of them pilots blows her quick, so she jest gives a squeak like a cat when you step on her, git off that boat as quick as you can. 'Cause that's a mean man, a smart-aleck man. The Lord don't like that kind of pilot, and he's going to sink that boat sure."

Ghosts have a special affinity for the packet boat. There is a famous spirit along the route of·the *Gordon C. Greene* whenever she plies between Cincinnati and Pittsburgh, known as the ghost of Mustapha Island. Many years ago a boat sank along this willowed stretch of the river and some of its passengers were drowned. The tragedy was only a few weeks old, when as a pilot was passing, he saw someone on shore waving a lantern. Believing it a signal, he steered the boat to land; but when he reached the shore, the light had oddly vanished. Thinking he was mistaken, he moved out to the river again. And instantly the light reappeared.

From that time to the present the mysterious light has showed each clear night with the regularity of the setting sun. At times it is like a flashlight; at times it is like a torch, or perhaps a man carrying a lantern. The skeptical of the region recall how years before the catastrophe, men searching for oil sunk a deep hole on the spot and abandoned the undertaking when the drill struck salt water; they declare the light is a will-o'-the-wisp, formed by marsh gas rising from the hole. But nevertheless, when they see the phantom, there is no laughter.

The roustabouts realize that a ghost must be treated with reverence and delicacy. "You got to be mighty polite with a ghost," Big Un told me, as he rested a moment between his labors of wheeling off coal for the boilers of the *Gordon Greene*. "If you're out in the country and got some whisky with you, don't git scared if the reins of the buggy you're a-riding in starts to jerking, or if it's a automobile, you hear the horn start blowing all by itself. It's jest a ghost a-wanting a drink. But you better git out and pour some whisky on the ground for him right away. And give him a good drink too, or you'll never git home again. If you're passing a graveyard a-chewing tobacco, and you hear something crying, kind of like a wildcat off in the swamps, only sad, don't let that

scare you neither. That's jest a ghost a-wanting a chew. Git
out the buggy, and walk to the graveyard fence, and put
down a nice big plug of tobacco. Next day if you pass it and
look, you'll see it's all kind of chewed up with the gum
marks of the ghost that's been a-working on it. And in a
couple of weeks or so, it'll all be gone away. You won't never
see no teeth marks. Jest gum marks. 'Cause there ain't no
kind of ghost that's ever got teeth, not even the ghost of a
dog. I was bit by a ghost once, on the arm. And it was like
you was being chewed by a banana."

The uses of these magical river beliefs are extensive. There
is always bad luck in the neighborhood, and if the river
dweller, on the boats or on the shore, is observant, and can
recognize the signs, he may be able to forestall disaster.
Spiders are among the best forewarners of tragedy. These
industrious insects write letters in their webs, which if
studied closely, may provide a significant message. The
spiders up the Cumberland and Tennessee Valleys warned
President McKinley again and again of his coming assassina-
tion, and wrote a large D for Death in every web they spun
around his picture. One old man rode off to Washington
and begged the President to be on his guard, but the Secret
Service men gave no heed. In 1914, the spiders all along the
Mississippi wrote huge W's everywhere; the war broke out
two weeks later. In 1929 hundreds of spiders wrote huge T's
standing for Trouble, but no one paid any attention, and
knocked the webs down with a stick. The spiders, knowing
what was to come, quietly wrote the letters in again.

Phenomena such as spider writing are of peculiar value,
because it is so easy to create bad luck. If two friends make
up the bed of a sick person, they can prepare at once for the
funeral. The patient will die. Or if a man watches a group

of departing friends, and does not turn away for an instant until they are out of sight, one of those friends will be lying in his grave before another moon has rolled on its way.

Magical information may be vital in that eternal problem of humanity, the matter of finding a mate. One warm summer afternoon on the *Tennessee Belle,* when the vessel was lying moored at the spice-scented wharf in New Orleans, and most of the crew had gone off to the town, Uncle Jesse, who had stayed behind for some duty, turned to me gravely. "Captain, I ain't seen you with no girl this trip," he declared. "Why don't you git yourself some of this come-here-to-me water? It's wonderful, this come-here-to-me water. When I gits ready to go uptown in New Orleans I puts a drop of it on my coat lapel, and when I walks on Canal Street, ain't a colored girl passes she don't turn her head. And the white people uses it a plenty, too. Every Friday night if you pass by them big New Orleans department stores you can see 'em taking big buckets of this come-here-to-me water and sprinkling it over the doorsteps. And Saturday morning there's such crowds in them stores you couldn't git a rooster inside. It's sure wonderful this come-here-to-me water."

With the proper knowledge, river magic may be made as valuable in securing money as finding the most attractive girls. One of the quickest methods is for the practitioner to find a rich man and contrive in some fashion to secure a lock of his hair. When this is accomplished let the maker of the spell bore a deep hole in an oak tree, put the hair inside, and plug it tightly with a piece of wood. He can now start spending his money recklessly, for his fortune is made. As long as the hair remains in the hole, the millionaire to whom it belongs will have headaches that drive him into frenzy.

Come-Here-to-Me Water

And when at last he learns the reason for his suffering, he will pay a king's ransom to gain relief.

I heard of a boy named David, living far up the mountain headwaters of the Tennessee, who applied his magical knowledge in practical fashion. Knowing how it is considered good luck to put a piece of silver under the bark of a tree, he would watch closely as his neighbors went into the woods to cut loose a piece of bark and slip a dime beneath. As soon as they had vanished, David would collect the dime.

But perhaps the easiest way to acquire a fortune, if the river dweller cares to take the risks, is to become a witch. Let the novice take a China dish and rifle, and climb a high hill just before dawn begins to streak the sky. Then, as the rim of the rising sun first touches the horizon, let him shoot the rifle three times and hold out the plate steadily before him. Soon three drops of blood will fall into the plate. Let him drink the blood slowly and when he has finished bring down curses on the head of the Lord, and chant praises to the Devil. And he can go home secure in his work of evil. For from that moment forth, he is a witch.

On the contrary, the river dweller may be one whose desire is not to become a sorcerer, but merely to be rid of those magicians who are making his life a burden. Humanity is often tormented by witches with no one aware of the true source of the misery. If the roustabout has been waking up suddenly in the night with bad dreams and a feeling of heavy pressure on his chest, this is not indigestion as some might think; it is a witch that has been using the luckless negro as a horse and riding him wildly over the countryside. And if the roustabout searches long enough in the bed clothes, he may find some of the burrs that clung to his clothing in his mad racing through the woods.

Fortunately there are means to counteract these creatures of darkness.

"You can stop a witch mighty easy," declared Uncle Jesse as he finished his toilet and made ready to join his fellows in New Orleans. "All you got to do is to git you a flour sifter or a piece of mosquito bar, and put it over your face jest before you go to bed. Witch has to go through every single one of them meshes before she can git to you, and ain't a witch can do it nowheres. 'Cause it gits dawn before she's anywheres near finished, and she's got to fly away. If you twist up little corners in the mosquito bar, sometimes you can catch 'em, 'cause when they git mighty tired they falls inside. They looks kind of like what they calls gelatin. If you ain't got a mosquito bar, throw down mustard seed. 'Cause a witch is out of her skin, and thataway the soles of her feet's terrible tender. Them mustard seeds 'd hurt her till she was crying if she walked on 'em; so she's got to pick up every one before she can git to work tormenting you. And by the time she's done got through, rooster's a-crowing."

Rivertown

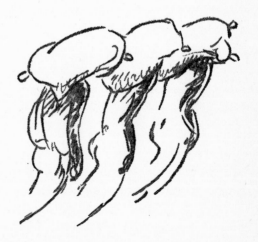

IX

SHADOWS ON A HILL

THE night was hot, and the air humid, oppressive, like the air before a storm. In the low-hanging sky the stars shone with extraordinary brilliance, like the fireflies twinkling everywhere over our heads; the planets and the golden insects were reflected again in dazzling constellations on the glassy surface on the river. From the darkness beyond the shore a whippoorwill called mournfully; somewhere in the shadows an owl hooted. At the water's edge frogs croaked deliriously.

The boat glided over the river, the huge barges before it creaking as they rounded a bend.

Suddenly the searchlight of the vessel flashed on, its beams piercing the blackness in a blinding circle. Starkly it silhouetted the twisting trunks of the cypress trees and their drooping boughs, hung everywhere with pendants of Spanish moss; beyond was a jungle, thick, impenetrable. An alligator at the water's edge, startled by the light, waddled off angrily into the protecting darkness. A water moccasin slid uglily off a log and disappeared in a pile of leaves. There were sounds of reeds crackling with the movements of some unseen animal, and curious rustlings. At times a mysterious vapor seemed to form and shroud the gnarled knees of the cypresses.

A towering negro emerged from the quarters of the deck hands and moved across the barges to take soundings. His voice echoed softly over the water. A great bird, roused from its sleep, flew up before him, flapping its wings; huge colored moths drifted like gaudy jewels into the rays of the searchlight. The calls of the leadsman ceased. The light went out.

Silently the barges drifted past the spectral trees. A dull glow appeared on the distant horizon. The shadowy figure standing near me in the blackness of the pilot house turned his head to look. He stood motionless a moment, then struck a match and lit the silver-rimmed pipe he was holding. The flame revealed a thin, dark face, with finely chiseled, aristocratic features, the face of an artist, perhaps a musician. His eyes, fixed on the horizon, were thoughtful, troubled.

"It's a city of ghosts," he said.

The vessel continued to move soundlessly along the edge of the swamp. A shanty boat lay at the bank; near it a man and a woman sat in a rowboat fishing. The towboat veered to avoid them.

The glow in the sky grew brighter. The man with the pipe continued to watch intently. "It's a city of ghosts," he repeated.

The glow vanished as the vessel rounded a bend, then reappeared brightly. The figure with the pipe smoked for a time in silence. "Sometimes they're charming ghosts. Lovely girls in hoop skirts dancing at a ball for some visitor from Europe, with gay music, and slaves hurrying about carrying drinks and delicacies to tempt the palates of the guests. And then suddenly everything changes and there are only malignant ghosts, like some grim story by Poe or Balzac: the ghosts of the War between the States, with all its destruction of beautiful homes and plantations, and the cruelty and ruined lives everywhere."

The whistle of the boat blew hoarsely. The man with the pipe kept silent until it had finished. He went on slowly. "And even when they are charming ghosts, there always seems about them an air of sadness, like a beautiful girl grown old while she waits for her lost lover.... I don't know. You can blame it all on the Yankees, I suppose. They won the war. We lost it. To the victor the spoils. Yet I don't condemn them. I'm not defending the system. It was fine for the man on top. Slaves for every whim. All the luxuries of Europe and the Orient, with every boat coming up the river bringing some expensive novelty for the pleasure of the masters and mistresses of the great houses. But I know it was bad for the man on the bottom, white as well as black. Only sometimes I think the North might have been . . . well . . . a little more . . . delicate. We've always been a sensitive people here. . . . Perhaps too sensitive for our own good."

The glow in the sky suddenly became the lights of a city atop a high hill. On the river bank at the foot of the bluff a string of other lights twinkled, climbing in a sharp angle toward the summit.

"Be there in five minutes," announced the quiet-spoken captain, standing beside us.

The man with the pipe nodded. He filled the bowl with tobacco, then spoke again in reflection. "I suppose it was the river did it too, as well as the Yankees. It was the river made us. Sailing vessels coming up from Turkey and China and India and any country you could think of. There are houses here that still have punkahs brought from Calcutta or Madras, so that a slave could swing them back and forth and keep the rooms cool in hot weather. And after the sailing ships the steamboats came, taking our cotton and sugar and rice everywhere. We were a big port in those days. There wasn't a sailor or riverman in the world who didn't know us. Then the river traffic died, and we died, too."

The vessel neared the land. With a heavy sighing of its smokestacks, it made fast to the dim-lit wharf. A short distance away some negro roustabouts were rolling bales of cotton toward a steamboat moored alongside, panting as they labored; from a row of negro shacks strung along the bank behind them came the raucous sounds of a mechanical piano.

The man with the pipe put on a broad-brimmed Panama that only partially concealed his long black hair. It threw his finely chiselled features into sharp relief.

With the captain, we descended, and walked across the barges to the shore. A bony dog skulked out from the weeds and sniffed suspiciously at our heels. A pig grunted sleepily in the distance. We neared the row of negro dwellings; the noise of the mechanical piano grew louder. Inside we could see some gaudily clad negresses and some negro men, playing cards. Out of the door there drifted a voice singing in hushed melancholy:

"Standing on de platform,
A-waiting for de train,
I'm going down to New Orleans
To wear de ball and chain."

We had been confined on the boat for several days; to stretch our legs we began to walk up the steep road. The man with the pipe looked back toward the shacks where the music of the piano still drifted faintly. "That's all there is left of Under the Hill," he said.

We climbed up the road, panting a little with the exertion and the oppressive air. Great trees, heavy-laden with their pendants of Spanish moss, towered above us like gloomy sentinels; across the river the ferryboat, waiting at the dark Louisiana shore, blew its whistle sharply, and began moving over the water. Some automobiles whisked past us on their way to meet it.

We halted a moment for breath. Absently my dark-haired companion polished the silver rim of his pipe with his finger. "All sorts of ghosts along this road," he declared. "Robust ghosts, mostly. Years ago this spot where we're walking was teeming with life. Negroes passing all day long, like ants, carrying bundles of wood on their heads to sell in town for a nickel or a dime. And down below, Under the Hill, steamboats were thick as bees about a sunflower." He brushed at a bat circling near us. "Blocks and blocks of houses for gambling and fancy women. And the place full of men who'd kill you for a drink of whisky. It was a real port, even if it was a river port. Like Aden, or Marseilles. Steamboat men were rough in those times. Not the gentlemen they are today. There's a story one of the biggest gambling houses kept a parrot sitting in a cage outside the door, yelling at everybody who passed: 'Come in, boys. Come in, girls. Only honest place Under the Hill.'"

The captain, a tall, stalwart man with a weather-beaten face, nodded. "Funny story, too, about the packet boat. The packet landed, and a passenger went ashore to do a little gambling, and had his pocket picked. It was all the money he had, a couple of hundred dollars, I guess, and he came back to the captain of the boat and told him about it. The

captain was a man with a pretty hot temper and he knew the
sheriff wouldn't or couldn't do anything about it. So he went
to the gambling house and asked for his passenger's money.
The proprietor just laughed at him. And the captain got excited. The gambling house was a rickety little place, built on
stilts, right at the water's edge, so the steamboaters wouldn't
have to walk more than a few feet to lose their money. The
captain fastened a big rope to one of the stilts and made the
other fast to the boat. Then he gave orders for the boat to
back away. It was a big steamboat, and in about a minute
the stilts began cracking, and the whole gambling house
started caving into the water. The passenger got his money
back."

We laughed. But our laughter seemed misplaced. A mysterious, brooding quality lay over the trees about us, as
though at any instant some spectral figure might step out
from between the trunks and challenge our right to passage.

We reached the top of the long slope now, with the river
winding far below us. A faint wind was blowing, and the
air was fresher. But there was no lessening of the brooding
quality, the mystery. The streets were deserted. The railroad
station, a short distance away, was dark, desolate, as though
no train had stopped before it since the day the troops of the
invading Northerners swept through the town. Some great
live oaks spread their wide branches before us, as though to
block out the bricked ugliness. We moved on again beyond
other shadowy trees, all looped with streamers of Spanish
moss, all resonant with the shrill singing of countless cicadas
and katydids. We passed some stately, white-porticoed houses,
their lofty columns misty in the starlight; the rich fragrance
of unseen tropical gardens touched our nostrils. A faint yellow light, as though a candle from some ancient time, ap-

peared behind a drawn curtain, for an instant illuminating the long veranda, where once fashionably clad swains with burnished pistols at their belts made love to dainty young women in crinolines.

The light flickered out.

The thin face of the man with the pipe grew thoughtful once more. "Ghosts. Nothing but ghosts. If these streets could speak, they'd cry out at the tragedies they witnessed. It wasn't a pleasant night when the poor negroes were freed all of a sudden after the Northern troops took the town. They didn't know what to do with this new wonderful thing they'd heard of called liberty. So they took up guns and bayonets and ran up and down like crazy men, looting and pillaging. They drank all the whisky in the hotel, and when

it was all finished, set the building on fire. And there was
the Yankee officer who mounted the beautiful horse belonging to the daughter of one of the town's prominent families.
The horse threw him. The officer got up from the ground,
whipped out his pistol, and shot the animal dead. And there
was the other Northern officer, who after the city's capture,
because someone forgot, wasn't invited to a party given in
a great house that was one of the beauties of the South. The
officer happened to be put in charge of building the Union
fortifications. He designed them so that they would pass
directly through the mansion. The engineers and their men
set to work. And in a few days nothing was left except a
desolate ruin. Even the colored people came and watched,
and had difficulty holding back their tears.... We'll find my
wife at the hotel."

We walked on a short distance. In the lobby of the hotel
was sitting a quietly dressed woman with the same delicate,
sensitive features that distinguished my dark-haired companion. We all climbed into the automobile waiting outside.
The car moved silently through the tree-lined streets, the
insects in the branches above us never ceasing their shrill
symphony. We drove down the main avenue now. Inter-
mingled with the gentry of the town here and there were
sad-faced women and girls, the wives and daughters of the
poorer white inhabitants of the region, come in from the
cotton plantations and the cypress swamps to buy a cheap
dress decorated with some gaudy jewelry or a brilliant colored photograph adorned with a huge gold frame.

We neared the negro section. The quiet-dressed woman
leaned toward her husband at the wheel. "Drive to Uncle
Lige," she said. She turned to me in explanation. "Lige is
a hundred and six years old."

We drove past some tiny negro churches, down a street crowded with black men and women. From the shabby doors of the poolrooms and barber shops there came occasionally the strains of a guitar or a banjo. We turned a corner into a narrow alley, and stopped before a neat cabin where some hollyhocks and sunflowers were growing. Here on a porch a little old negro was sitting. His face was wrinkled like a walnut shell; when he arose to greet us, his movements were so stiff, the crackling of the rickety chair in which he had been sitting might easily have been mistaken for the creaking of his bones. Yet despite his age his eyes were bright; his face was still gay, animated.

"Sure, I seen the race, Captain," he murmured in answer to a question when he had feebly taken a seat once more. "It was a wonderful race. People a-standing along the banks like chickens at feeding time, a-yelling and hollering. And the *Natchez* and the *Robert E. Lee* with big flames coming out their smokestacks like a sawmill on fire. I looked at them two boats a-roaring up the river and then I looked at the water. 'Fish, you better go to the bottom,' I says."

He shifted creakily in his chair. "I seen a plenty of other boats, too. I seen the first steamboat come down the river with these here electric wires on her. She done had one of them big searchlights, and it was sure a-flashing terrible. Never been one on the river no-ways. And all the niggers gits to yelling and a-dropping to their knees. 'Cause they figured it was judgment day, and God was a-coming down the river, picking out the good people from the bad."

There was a question from the lady now. The old negro turned quickly to her. "Yes'm, I worked for him, Miss Lucy. Over in the white house by them cottonwoods. There was some mighty fine times over in the white house. Bad times, too when they whipped you. But there wasn't no sin like there is today. Today there ain't nothing but sin." With the cheap palm leaf fan he was holding he slapped at a great June bug wheeling clumsily near him. "There was eight hundred slaves, I reckon, over yonder. Most of 'em was a-working out in the cotton fields. But there was a plenty in the house too. I was always a-working in the house. I never was no field nigger." He cracked the fan sharply against the arm of his chair, in pursuit of the blundering insect. "It was sure pretty in the white house. There was a fine bell for every nigger. Each of 'em sounded different, too. Jest like they was steamboat whistles. One of 'em 'd go kind of high, mink-a-mink. That was old Rebecca's bell. One of 'em 'd go kind of deep, chung-a-chung. That was old Amos' bell. My bell 'd go kind of mixed up someways, mink-a-chung, mink-a-chung. When it'd ring—you better be there."

We talked a while, fanning ourselves constantly in the hot July night. We rose to go.

The lady spoke quietly again.

The old negro turned in slight indignation. "Course I done fought in the war, Miss Lucy. I done fought on the side of them gray soldiers. Then old Master went away and I seen his side was a-losing. So I quit a-fighting with them gray soldiers and done begun fighting with the blue.... It's a mighty funny thing. Jest one of 'em 'll give me what they calls a pension. I done tried plenty of times, but I can't git it from both of 'em no-ways."

We climbed into the car and drove away.

We were in the country now. At times we passed some beautiful old house faintly visible behind its protecting live oaks. Great trees were everywhere about us; occasionally they grew closer and closer at the top, until at last they met, transforming the highway into a mysterious green tunnel. Now and then a cotton wagon bumped past us, its old negro driver sleeping over the reins, while the rickety horse before him plodded drowsily on its way.

We saw the river again in the distance, a golden ribbon now in the huge yellow moon which had climbed above the horizon. We disembarked, and were walking through some high grass, when we halted suddenly. The earth before us had ended. We were standing on the brink of a gigantic precipice, its walls curving out on both sides of us to form a vast circular pit, like the crater of an enormous volcano. Far below we could vaguely discern the bottom, tangled, touched with wisps of mist like phantoms. Curious whisperings seemed to arise from it, like the voices of unearthly animals.

The dark-haired man walked close to the brim. "It's the Devil's Punch Bowl," he said.

He stood motionless, watching. "More ghosts here," he added. "Sinister ghosts." He knocked the ashes from his pipe and polished the silver rim with his finger once more. "Nobody knows what caused the Punch Bowl. Some say it's the river. Some say it was a queer kind of earthquake. Some say it was a meteor. I've heard rivermen swear that the needle of the compass goes crazy when a steamboat passes here. Whatever the cause, it's had a grim history."

His foot chanced to touch a loose clump of earth. The clay went rattling down the slope, like the beat of some far-off drum. He spoke again. "God knows how many people were murdered here in the old days. River pirates made it their headquarters. They'd have lookouts here on the high land, and when they sighted flatboats coming, they'd go out to raid them. Then they'd come back to the swamp down

Old Slave

below us to divide the spoils. But the worst thing was the slave uprising. Murrell, the bandit, had his headquarters here. He and his leaders decided that the best way to rob the rich houses in the neighborhood would be to start a revolt of the negroes. In the confusion, the bandits could dash up and steal anything they wanted. It was a fine plan, worked out to the last detail. Certain slaves on each planta-tion were assigned to kill their masters and every member of his family. But the plot was discovered when a negress wouldn't promise to kill the white child she was nursing. What followed wasn't...pretty."

We drove into the night again. The trees closed over our heads once more and blotted out the sky. A house with lofty white columns showed in the moonlight. The car came to a stop. We walked beneath the towering pillars onto a wide veranda and went through the door into a hallway hung with portraits. An elderly woman with a gentle face and dreamy blue eyes that seemed to be gazing into some distant world came forward to greet us. With her silvery hair and slightly old-fashioned costume, she might have stepped a moment before from one of the fading portraits on the wall. She led us into a living room where three charmingly dressed young women were sitting. More portraits hung here in profusion; each piece of furniture was a costly heirloom. The room was a veritable museum. Yet it had none of the museum's stiffness. It was warm, livable.

We sat talking pleasantly, drinking lemonade from tall crystal glasses. I remarked about the stately beauty of the house.

The silvery-haired hostess smiled with pleasure. Then her face was touched with sadness. "I suppose our houses are all we have left." She sipped her drink slowly, staring into the

bottom as though she saw there the pageant of some vanished era. "It must have been pleasant in many ways, the
old life. The slaves everywhere, and money like the wealth
of Midas. But I know it couldn't go on forever. Life changes.
I'm getting to be an old woman now, and I think differently
about a number of things I would have died for when I was
a girl. You have plenty of time to think, living in one of
these old houses."

She stirred her glass dreamily. "Mother used to tell me
there was so much money here one man built a stable with
enormous mirrors in the stalls so his horses could stand in
front of the glasses and preen themselves all day long. They
say the horses used to act just like a young woman waiting
for her first beau."

A faint wind wafted into the room the perfume of flowers
in the garden beyond the window.

She breathed deep of the delicate fragrance. "I suppose
I could sell the house and move to New Orleans or Washington or New York and be in the midst of things. But to
me there's something sacred about a home like this one,
that was my mother's house and my great-grandmother's
house before me. Here I'm content to sit and look out over
the camellias and the crepe myrtle in the garden, and think
of the days when we were in our glory. In this house I have
memories. And perhaps memories are all that people growing old have left."

We departed soon after, and walking under the towering
pillars that framed the doorway, drove off between the
stately trees that fringed the road. We reached the top
of the hill overlooking the wharf. Below us our boat lay
twinkling on the water. It whistled mournfully. The car
turned down the hill toward it.

At the river bank, the roustabouts were still loading cotton. From the negro shacks along the bank there occasionally came the sound of a mechanical piano and the voice of a negro singing in melancholy:

"O police captain, give me coffee and a bed,
Open up your jailhouse. 'Cause I shot a nigger dead."

My dark-haired companion bade good-by to his wife. We walked with the captain onto the towboat. The vessel whistled and started moving down the water.

A negro standing at the rail turned to me wistfully. "Captain, you ain't got a dime a kind of laying loose in your pants pocket, has you? The niggers here can git all your money quicker than a fox can steal a frizzly chicken."

The lights of Natchez grew fainter and fainter.

The boat glided soundlessly along the spectral trees that formed the shore. From the tall reeds came mysterious rustlings. The frogs croaked softly.

We rounded a bend. The dull glow in the sky grew fainter and fainter.

The shadowy figure beside me took out his silver-rimmed pipe and lit a match. "It's a city of ghosts," he said.

Long Voyage

Ead's Bridge, St. Louis

X

THE PIONEERS: ST. LOUIS TO THE TWIN CITIES

WE'RE pioneers," said the wistful-faced little man in excitement as the *Golden Eagle* made ready to leave the St. Louis wharf. "I tell you we're sure pioneers. Hasn't been a steamboat go from St. Louis to St. Paul in twenty-five years. It's a mighty big day for the river."

The tart old man with a cane sitting near him grunted wrathfully. "She'll never make St. Paul if she takes seventy-five years. Packet boating's done for on the river. There's twenty-six locks and all those drawbridges she's got to squeeze through. And even if she gets through 'em, she'll never pass Lake Pepin. Nobody ever gets past Pepin. It's the steamboat graveyard."

The wistful little man looked troubled. "She'll make it. She's got to make it. There's going to be crowds waiting all the way to St. Paul. They were saying up in Wabasha if she makes it they're going to spend fifty million dollars on new steamboat lines. River 'll be full of boats, going all the time. If she don't make it, the Government's going to close up all the locks and dams and just let 'em have the river for fishing, they say."

Captain Buck, the genial giant who was the vessel's owner, took his black cigar from his mouth, and called a command. There was an answering shout below. The tattered negro roustabouts began to loose the mooring lines.

A quiver of excitement ran through the crowd watching on the bank. Hats and handkerchiefs waved gaily; whistles on the near-by towboats blew hoarsely.

"It's a big day, Captain Buck," shouted a hatless figure on the bank. "We'll all be watching you. They'll be watching you from Maine to California. If you make it, this 'll be the biggest thing in the Valley since the flood of '83."

"She's the *Golden Eagle*. She'll live up to her name," answered Captain Buck quietly.

The whistle blew. The vessel began to move slowly from the wharf.

Captain Buck puffed at his cigar. "Looks like we're off," he said.

Under the bridges we sped, while the passengers crowded about the railings, and waved wherever a sign of life showed on the craft that went tooting past us. The smokestacks coughed softly, hypnotically.

A pretty girl wearing a bright green dress and vivid earrings looked anxiously about the deck. "When does the dancing start?" she demanded. "I don't like a trip unless there's dancing."

The smoke of St. Louis became a gray cloud on the horizon. Past riverlight on riverlight we glided, and saw the muddy Missouri, long the curse of rivermen, too thin to cultivate, too thick to navigate.

A faint bell rang, and we sat down to eat our dinner.

Captain Buck arose hastily from the table. "We're coming to the first lock at Alton," he said. "I'll have to watch it."

He went outside. Quietly he spoke to the negroes waiting below with their heavy lines. The vessel neared the towering walls of the dam against which it might suddenly shatter as a piece of china breaks on a stony sidewalk, then glided slowly past. A great metal gate shut mysteriously behind us. There was a thunderous hissing of water; in a moment we were rising as if by magic over the countryside. A new gate opened before us now; the boat moved forward.

Some automobiles had dashed down the bank and halted, honking their horns noisily. A lock tender wearing a yellow life preserver strolled to the water's edge.

"It's a big day, Captain Buck!" he shouted.

Darkness fell, a hot, summer darkness. Stars shone in silvery radiance. On the shore fireflies gleamed in a twinkling curtain, as though in some curious fashion they had become part of the star-studded sky. The cities were far behind us now. In the distance a train whistled sadly. The strains of the orchestra that was playing within the cabin seemed muted, melancholy. On the prow of the boat, darkened so that the pilot above might better see his way, men and women stood without speaking, awed by the majesty of the river night.

Captain Buck sat in a canvas armchair, smoking his black cigar in meditation. "It's a strange river," he said. "Never know what new trick it's going to have ready for you. Never lets you rest. But I guess it's better than steamboating in the old days like up on the Missouri where they used to put boiler plate around the pilot houses to keep off the bullets of the Indians. This upper Mississippi where we're heading was all Indian country. Plenty of scalping and buffaloes. The mother and father of the pilot that's on watch now went out a little way into the West and lived for years just collecting the buffalo bones that were lying on the prairie and sending them East for fertilizer. Their son didn't like an easy life, though. He wanted to be a riverman, and steer a packet where one hadn't been in twenty-five years.... You'd better have one of these cigars. Nothing like a good cigar when you're steamboating."

He was called away soon after, and I went below. A dozen tattered roustabouts were stretched out on benches, sleeping. One lean negro, with a long scar marring his bony cheek, sat on a nail-keg intoning phrases from a ragged Bible. It was Good Book Johnny, the roustabout preacher.

There came a sudden burst of music from the orchestra above us.

Good Book Johnny listened. His gaunt face grew gloomy. "Lord's a-going to strike 'em dead," he murmured. "Ain't nothing but music and dancing. Ain't nothing in the world today but sin."

He preached to me solemnly. A withered negro named Old Gabe sat and nodded silent assent.

Suddenly there was a curious buzzing about our ears; the air became thick with willow bugs, those huge, floundering insects of the upper river born to live only a few moments, says legend, because a cruel nature created them without mouths to eat.

The winged invasion increased. The lights were blotted out. Our eyes, our nostrils seemed filled with fluttering wings. Suddenly the lights shone bright again. The fluttering ceased. But on the floor lay a thick carpet formed by thousands of the motionless bodies. Some negroes went about with shovels pushing the yellow masses into the river.

Good Book Johnny watched gravely. "Them's the sons of Canaan," he said. "They've done been cursed by the Lord."

I went upstairs again. We were near a town now. A long parade of automobiles was following us, their headlights flashing, their horns blowing raucously.

The wistful little man waved toward the unseen drivers and beamed with excitement. "I tell you, we're sure pioneers. It said in the St. Louis paper today we're opening up a new wonderland, and that's sure right. The upper Mississippi's the most wonderful scenery in the world. I can prove it, too." He hurried off breathlessly to his cabin, and returned in a moment with a cheap little camera whose surface was entirely hidden by labels. "Look at those labels. You see that one, tincture of iodine? I got that in a drugstore in Pueblo, Colorado. And you see that label, essence of peppermint? That came from a drugstore in Omaha. I've been everywhere. Some of the labels came from lunch stands, too. That label's from Jake's Eat Place in Dallas. I guess that proves it to you. The upper Mississippi's the most beautiful scenery in the world."

"If you get there to see it," said the tart old man with the cane. "She won't get past the big dam at Keokuk. And even if she does, there's plenty of pioneers in the bottom of Lake Pepin. Pepin's what they call the Storm Kettle. Makes the storms for the whole United States. When they get a bad tornado in Arkansas, or a blizzard way off in New York or those places, everybody knows it came from Pepin."

I stayed awake till long after the other passengers had gone to bed, watching the black smokestacks travel across the sky. I arose to go off to my cabin. I saw a giant figure at the bow, and the glowing end of a cigar. It was Captain Buck, alert, watchful, his eyes fixed on the dark water before him.

The Golden Eagle

I went to sleep. Once I awakened as the boat blew for a
lock. Vaguely I could hear the voice of the captain, and the
answering shouts of the negroes as they tossed their hempen
lines. The boat swayed faintly in its stony chamber and rose
like a ghost into the night.

I heard a voice call cheerfully: "Hope you make it, Captain Buck."

I awakened early in the morning. Low hills formed the
shores now, with here and there a rocky cliff overhanging
the water. The bridge that marked Hannibal came into view.
I went ashore and strolled along the streets where the young
Sam Clemens had wandered; visited the rambling old house
which had been his home. It was a gentle, sleepy little city
as was fitting, with soft-spoken, friendly inhabitants, and
friendly, slightly dilapidated dogs going leisurely down the
sidewalks on their various errands. There were automobiles;
but they seemed a little frightened, and anxious to remain
in the background. For like the rusty dogs, and the mules
and horses ambling along the quiet streets, they knew that
an automobile was a crude interloper in this famous river
town.

I made my way back to the river. A lazy figure clad in
faded shirt and trousers sat on the bank, holding a home-
made fishing rod. He brightened as I came near. "Did you
see the shoe factory?" he drawled amiably. "You sure ought
to see the shoe factory. She's the best anywheres in the world,
everybody says. You can eat a piece of cake off the floor of
that shoe factory. It's the finest thing to see in Hannibal."

Up the river we glided once more, and came in sight of
Quincy, tranquil, dignified, with a boat store on the bank
where the shanty fishermen came to buy their huge hoop

nets. A short distance away was a pleasant little park, where even the squirrels coming down from the trees seemed to have acquired the calm philosophy of the river, for they took their nuts like stately, unhurried gentlemen, instead of with the snatching eagerness that is their usual custom.

We went into a lock again. The lock wall was crowded now. Mothers stood holding their babies. Boys with dogs looked on excitedly. The river bank was becoming a vast auditorium, with the river the stage, and the boat the solitary player in the never-ending spectacle of man's battle to conquer the earth and the water.

A weather-beaten farmer waved a newspaper where a picture of the boat was plainly visible. "We're all watching you, Captain Buck," he shouted, as the rising water for a moment brought us on a level with the spectators. "They're talking about you in New York and everywhere."

The prow headed into the open water.

Boats of fishermen were frequent now; flatboats with over-alled rustics seeking catfish, and the curious craft of the mussel pearlers, resembling giant spiderwebs. Expertly the boatmen pried open the mussels and searched within for pearls; the shells they sent to factories up the river, where they would be transformed into buttons for the shirts of some Broadway stroller in the East.

I went up to the pilot house. Captain Jack, a towering man, with flashing blue eyes and a fiery temper, swung the vessel violently to avoid crashing into a squat Diesel boat which came charging suddenly forward. He cursed hotly. "These Diesel boats 'll kill me yet," he grunted.

"I'm going where I never see a Diesel boat," he went on a moment later, as his anger vanished. "Down on the Amazon, and run one of the Mississippi boats they've got working down there. Lot of pilots I know have done it. You remember old Glass Eye, used to be a pilot on the Lee Line at Memphis? He's down on the Amazon now, having a wonderful time. Got the steamboat people to tell the natives he was a god, and after a crowd of 'em collected on the banks, he went in swimming. He dived, and when he was under water, he took out his glass eye and came up holding it in his hand. When the natives were trying to figure that out, he dived under again, and when he came up this time, the eye was back in place. The natives fell on their knees and worshipped him. They thought he was the biggest god they'd ever seen. Glass Eye never does a lick of work any more. Just sits in a big straw house and the Indians bring him squab and wild turkey and the prettiest girls there are for miles around. I think I'll get my eye put out some way."

All day we proceeded between the gently sloping shores. The older passengers sat on the deck, chatting and watching the ever-changing panorama. The more youthful sat in secluded corners, making love. Great birds drifted before us; once an eagle crossed the bow, flying in solitary splendor.

The bell rang for the evening meal. I walked with Captain Buck to the dining room. "Eating's one of the fine things on a steamboat," he said. "I like to feed my passengers right. But seems like people don't eat the way they used to. It used to be terrible on a boat I knew that ran up in the tributaries. There was a man that was carpenter on her would eat a dozen eggs for breakfast. Eat them hard boiled in the shell, shell and all. Just put salt and pepper on the outside and swallow 'em whole. And the passengers were worse. Big lumberjacks from up around the head of the river. They'd eat fifteen flapjacks and three or four big steaks at a meal. The boat was crowded and they used to have two or three sittings, and the lumberjacks 'd try to come and eat a meal each time. The purser caught on to 'em though. After they'd eaten, he'd mark a big X on their backs with chalk, and by the time they got it rubbed off, the meals 'd be all over."

We finished and the orchestra began to play for the dancing. Darkness spread over the river. We neared the dam at Keokuk, the highest on the Mississippi, towering like a prison wall in the blackness, with its colored lights blinking an eerie warning to all who might approach. The pilot blew the whistle. But there came no answering signal from the great shadow before us. The massive gate that I could faintly see remained rigid, immovable. Minutes passed. Still the gate did not open.

The tart old man with the cane grew triumphant. "They're not going to let us through," he grumbled. "I told you we wouldn't get any further than Keokuk. This packet boat can't get in that lock. They know it. And they're not going to let her through."

As he spoke there was a creaking of machinery, and the huge gate, like the jaws of some fabulous water creature, opened before us. The vessel moved gingerly forward, like a hesitant animal feeling its way over treacherous ground. Higher and higher we rose. Vaguely we could see some shadowy figures on the lock wall below us.

"We're betting on you, Captain Buck," a deep voice shouted. "If you make it, river's going to be fuller of boats than the Panama Canal."

The tart old man with the cane grew stern. "She won't get past Pepin," he grunted.

The glow of the city faded behind us.

We saw the lights of Nauvoo, where the Mormons set out on their dreary exodus to the West.

It grew late. The dancing ceased. The passengers went off to bed, except the young lovers sitting silent in the darkness. The moon came out, and hung over the horizon like the glistening golden ball suspended as an ornament between the stacks of a steamboat. The air seemed to be changing now; it was dryer, clearer, with a tang like the starry nights over the St. Lawrence in Canada. We were moving north.

Lights glowed on the horizon again, and a bridge loomed before us. We were at Burlington, busy little city of Iowa, full of bright-cheeked country girls. The bridge creaked open to let us pass. A train waiting on the shore whistled in wrath.

My watch showed two, then three. I went off to my cabin. I opened the door, and stepped to my berth to take up my pajamas. I started back in astonishment. The berth was occupied. I looked closer. It was the wistful little man, sleeping blissfully. My movements roused him. He rubbed his eyes.

"Guess I must be getting kind of absent-minded," he said.

He shuffled off dazedly to his stateroom.

I stepped onto the deck outside my cabin for a final glance at the starlit valley. In the canvas armchair at the bow I saw Captain Buck's cigar still glowing as he sat intently watching the water. He had not gone to bed for two days.

The river was bathed in dazzling sunlight when I awakened. Mussel pearlers were drifting idly along the water; fishermen were pulling up the gleaming catches of their nets to send off to the nearby towns. Occasionally a shantyboat was moored along the shore, with a sunbonneted woman bent over a tub and a drab-clad girl hanging clothes on a line. We passed Muscatine, center of the mussel pearlers and the button factories.

The wistful little man came hurrying to me. His face was troubled. "I've lost my fountain pen," he said. "It was a wonderful fountain pen. It had labels on it like the camera. And it had a little hole in the top where you looked through and saw a picture of Niagara Falls. I can't find it anywhere."

On we steamed, the stacks sighing rhythmically. We halted at Rock Island, almost in the shadow of the great arsenal. The chimneys of many factories rose in the distance; beyond lay the smoke of Moline and across the river was Davenport. But there were few signs of cities or industry on the water-front. Some giggling girls bantered with a jovial boatman who was exhibiting some fish floundering in a bucket. A lanky, bronzed figure stood beside a weather-beaten fish dock waiting with his fresh-caught catfish for a passing customer. The shore was Illinois; but it might have been the levee of some hamlet in far distant Mississippi or Arkansas. Even in a super-mechanical age, a river invests cities and men with the simple and the elemental.

Three ragged urchins stood watching the rousters make the vessel fast. They hurried forward as Captain Buck appeared a moment on the gangplank.

"Everybody's watching you, Captain Buck," their leader declared in excitement. "Me and these two boys is all river-men. We help some of the mussel catchers. If you get to St. Paul it'll be a wonderful thing for the river."

I took the ferry across to Davenport, strolling about the streets of the scholarly little city, famous for its culture and its river captains, until the *Golden Eagle* blew an imperious blast of her whistle.

In a few moments I was aboard once more, watching the pilot steer the vessel through a narrow drawbridge. He cursed and swung the boat sharply to avoid a mussel fisherman darting directly in his path. "I don't know why anybody's a pilot.

If you're a pilot on a packet boat like this one, you have to shave every minute, and keep your pants pressed so that you could peel an apple with the crease, and all day long women ask you crazy questions. If you're a towboat pilot, with no women around, you never press your pants, and you get so lonesome for the sight of a girl, you'd pretty near kiss a billboard. I'm going to quit piloting and go to work in a restaurant."

"You won't work in a restaurant," declared Captain Buck in a calm voice. "You'll be at a wheel till you die. Then you can get yourself buried the way that old captain did down the valley. Had a beautiful stone tomb built on a hill by the river with a little window in it and his coffin standing straight up, so he could look out and curse all the steamboats going by."

The bell rang for dinner. When we finished, night had fallen. I went below to talk to the roustabouts. Good Book Johnny was sitting with his torn Bible, talking to old Gabe and gloomily watching some tattered negroes as they played coon-can. "Lord's a-going to strike 'em dead," he muttered. "Card playing and whisky and women is all them St. Louis niggers knows. Ain't no good trying to preach to nobody from St. Louis. Lord's a-going to strike St. Louis down."

"Only church a St. Louis nigger 'll go to is a hoodoo church, to git a Tobey so he can win money gambling," declared the wrinkled old Gabe in a quavering voice.

"Sure wish you could get me a good Tobey," sleepily mumbled Stockyard Sam, a fat negro who had been dozing near us. "I used to have a wonderful Tobey. I got it when I was working down in Natchez. I went out in them swamps and there was a old man living in a big hole under some cypresses. There was three nigger girls living there, too, taking care of him, cause he was terrible old. He never seen the sun for nine years, the girls said. Jest stayed down in the hole all the time. I told him what I wanted and he started talking kind of funny, and three big cottonmouth snakes come sliding in, with bells all around their necks, going tink-a-tink. They wrapped all around his neck and kissed him, and then a purple light come on all of a sudden. And the old man said: 'It's all right now. Give me your money.' I told him I jest had two dollars. And he took that and said I could pay him the rest when I earned it with the Tobey, ten cents for every dollar I took in. I went out, and I jest won money wonderful. And I sent him the ten cents on each dollar like he said. But then I got to kind of forgetting, and didn't send the money no more. And one night I was winning, pretty nearly a hundred dollars, and I was holding the Tobey tight. When all of a sudden it blowed up like dynamite, and burned my hand to the bone. And I knowed then he had made it turn against me, and I couldn't win no more. I went back to the swamp to find him, to give him the money. But where the hole used to be wasn't nothing now, jest a old screech owl hollering and laughing at me. I sure wish I'd have sent him them ten cents for the dollar."

The boat neared a lock. The negroes arose to take up the lines. From the deck above came the strains of the orchestra and the shuffling of the feet of the dancers.

Good Book Johnny listened. "Lord's a-going to punish 'em. He's a-going to punish all the dancers, and the gamblers. He's a-going to destroy the world."

A crowd was on the lock now, larger than any which had greeted us before. Bearded old men, who obviously never left their homes except on rare occasions, stood leaning on their canes, and watched in wonder. Automobiles were massed thickly behind them. An old woman with a fine, delicate face and a dress of a previous generation came down to the boat holding by the hand a tight-starched little girl. "I saw the last boat go through, twenty-five years ago, Captain," she said in a soft voice. "And I wanted my granddaughter to see you today. If you get to St. Paul, it's going to make history."

We glided out of the lock gates.

The scenery was changing now. The bluffs were growing higher.

The wistful little man hurried to me, his face ecstatic. "It's coming," he burst out. "It's the most beautiful scenery in the world."

The bluffs became great shadowy cliffs seeming ready at each instant to topple into the river and overwhelm us. The world became mysterious, eerie. Fantastic shapes, like brooding gods, showed against the black horizon. Above them the stars shone with unnatural brightness. This was a far different stream than the lower river, with its gleaming sandbars and its swamps and its alligators. This was the castle-crowned Danube, winding its way through the mountains to the Black Sea. We had reached the Mississippi Palisades.

A long time I sat, reflecting on the vastness of this ever-changing river, then went off to my cabin.

Often during the night I could hear the honking of belated automobiles following us along the bank, and could see the flashing patterns of their headlights as they pierced the starry sky.

In the morning monastery-bordered Dubuque came in sight, high on the bluffs. We went ashore, and at the top of the highest hill looked out over the valley. A green wilderness lay far below us; through it the river ran like a silvery thread, seeming as virgin as in the days when the canoes of the Indians and the French explorers first glided over its glassy surface. There were no feathered Indians now and no French explorers. But their traces were everywhere, in the legends and in the names of the settlements.

We steamed on our way.

I passed the wistful little man standing in the door of his cabin. Inside I could see the black maid busily turning the mattress upside down and searching under the floor. "We can't find the fountain pen anywhere," he told me in distress. "It's a wonderful fountain pen. When you look at the hole in the top backwards from the regular way you see what they call the Cave of the Winds."

We passed Guttenberg with its odd Germanic buildings, and came in sight of McGregor, picturesque settlement lying at the edge of the towering cliffs that bordered the river. Here in a little store was a gentle old man almost hidden by the shimmering mussel shells piled in profusion all about him, a venerable figure who, the natives said, was the largest buyer of fresh-water pearls in America. I had often heard how, when a particularly beautiful pearl was discovered in the river, buyers would come to bid on it even from the Orient; and it was curious to reflect that the Mississippi pearls in this little shop in Iowa might some day grace the crown of some beautiful olive-skinned Maharanee of Indore or princess of Assam.

Past Prairie du Chien we drifted, once the bustling wilderness metropolis where the fur traders came to buy skins from the Indians and the white hunters, but now only a hushed, ghostly little town living on its memories.

We had arrived in the heart of the Indian country now.

Night fell. We glided through a lock. An old man wearing a high-throated collar and a flowing black tie walked feebly to the prow. "I was one of the pilots on the last boat through, Captain Buck. My wife went to church last night to pray that you can make it to St. Paul."

The mystery of the country increased. The boat seemed excited, nervous now, as though it were frightened in the brooding darkness. The sighing of the stacks was troubled. The bluffs took the shape of great fortresses; stony giants crouched at their feet, as though they were guarding the spirits of the Indians killed in the bloody battles with the white men.

Captain Buck chewed his cigar. "Used to be a lot of Indian steamboat pilots. Half-breeds really. French and Indian. Made wonderful pilots. Most of them were proud of their Indian blood. But there was one pathetic case, a fellow they called Indian Bill. He went steamboating down one of the tributaries where the crew made fun of him all the time. Said an Indian could only run a steamboat as long as he had somebody to give him orders. Indian Bill was a fine pilot, but after a while it got so all the talking shook his confidence. One day the captain got sick and asked him to take charge. Indian Bill tried to get out of it. But the captain said he wasn't coming on this trip. Said Bill could steer every inch of the way blindfolded. The boat started out, with the Indian in charge of her. And she hadn't been gone ten minutes when he wrecked her on a rock that he knew as well as he knew his little finger. He never touched a wheel after that."

We neared a little town. The pretty girl in the green dress and the vivid earrings watched as she leaned on the arm of the pleasant-faced youth beside her. "It's beautiful here," she remarked. "I've come through driving. There's a fine place for dancing. It has a wonderful floor."

When I awakened the next day the country had begun to change again. The hills were growing lower and moving back from the river. On both sides of us now were the rich farms and pastures of Wisconsin and Minnesota. Sleek cattle grazed near the water's edge.

I went up to the pilot house. The pilot was watching the sky intently. "We'll be getting to Pepin about dark," he said. "If we get any weather there it's going to be bad."

We glided into a lock again. A fat, ruddy-faced figure standing in the crowd called out jovially: "We're betting on you, Captain Buck. Just a hundred and twenty-five miles to go."

The boat seemed to be moving faster.

We stopped at Winona, rich little town with its imposing bank adorned, as its inhabitants proudly boast, by the two largest columns quarried from a single block of marble in the entire universe. We passed Fountain City, tiny but gay settlement where, legend says, the happy natives drink their wine with such gusto that when a man has only a hundred gallons remaining he sadly announces his cellar is empty.

Into another lock we glided. A voice came from beyond the lock wall: "Only eighty-seven miles to go, Captain Buck."

I returned to the pilot house. The pilot was watching the sky anxiously again, where some feathery clouds showed in the West. "We'll be at Pepin pretty soon," he declared.

On we steamed. In the distance we could dimly see the lake now, silent, melancholy.

The sun set redly. The feathery clouds gathered round it like the plumes on some gigantic hearse. The sighing of the stacks became quick, nervous, like the breathing of a frightened animal.

We steamed into the lake as darkness descended; saw stretched out before us that vast, mysterious pool over twenty miles long and three miles wide into which the river is suddenly transformed, a Mississippi incredible to one who has known only the levee-hemmed waters of Louisiana and Arkansas.

I went below with the roustabouts.

The black plumes in the sky that marked the vanished sun grew thicker, ominous.

Good Book Johnny watched them gloomily. "The Lord's a-going to destroy the world," he muttered. "He's going to destroy it like Canaan's children. With a cloud from the palm of his hand."

The negroes near him ceased their card playing and fixed their eyes on the dark horizon.

A navigation light on the shore shone wanly. The fat face of Stockyard Sam grew grave. "There's seven of them shiny lights we got to pass on by. We won't be all right till them seven shiny lights is behind us, and a-looking the other way."

The throbbing of the engines quickened. The wheel spun faster. The boat shook with the vibration. The deckboards rattled like beating drums.

"Listen to her talking," murmured a young negro standing rigid at the railing. "She smells all them dead boats laying in the water."

Old Gabe, who was near him, shuddered. "It's them dead Indians makes all the storms. They says there's a Indian comes off the mountain riding a big black horse. It's him that brings the wind."

The feathery plumes of cloud merged at the base, and became long, twisting arms, like the tentacles of a huge octopus.

We were in a lost world now. The shores were far in the distance, like mountainous islands. This was no longer a steamboat; we were on a sailing ship, voyaging through some mysterious sea.

Stockyard Sam stared hypnotically into the distance. "One light gone," he droned.

A black tentacle of the cloudy octopus overhead stretched further and further across the water. "It's going to storm," mumbled Good Book Johnny. "The hand of the Lord's going to wipe out sin."

The boat swayed faintly.

Old Gabe shivered again. "Let her through, Lord. This here boat's the *Golden Eagle,* Lord. Let her fly through."

Silence fell over the watchers at the rail.

"Two lights gone," droned Stockyard Sam.

The black tentacle of cloud reached nearer. But still there came no wind. Stray wisps of fog rose here and there over the water, assuming shapes like fluttering ghosts. Some great birds, roused by the approach of the vessel, flew past the prow, flapping their wings noisily. Huge white moths floated before us, brushing our faces. Tall reeds lined our path where the water grew shallow, and waved uneasily; curious circular plants like giant water lilies bobbed up and down eerily as we passed.

"Four lights gone," droned the fat negro.

We passed some stunted trees, drowning in the water that reached halfway up their melancholy trunks; there came a smell of dank, rotting vegetation.

On we sped, the towering smokestacks racing against the

St. Paul

sky. Another great tentacle of cloud twisted out to join the first.

"Six lights gone," droned Stockyard Sam.

From above there drifted the faint sound of the orchestra and the shuffling of feet in a waltz. The music seemed to have an unearthly quality, as though there were no musicians, no dancers, only a spectral orchestra playing for some disembodied spirits doomed to float forever on this phantom sea.

The tentacles of cloud began to writhe angrily now. The boat swayed uneasily once more. The engines beat feverishly. The sighing of the stacks became a frenzied panting.

"Let her through, Lord," murmured old Gabe. "She's the *Golden Eagle*, Lord. Let her fly through."

Suddenly a light appeared before us, dazzling in the ghostly darkness. We headed toward it, and quickly steamed past.

It was the light at the head of the lake. We were across.

On the boat sped, eagerly, triumphantly now, like the weary horse who knows that the stable marking his journey's end is near. A long shadow emerged from the darkness, and we saw a yacht, graceful-lined, luxurious. There came a muffled hail.

"Ahoy the *Golden Eagle!* We've come to meet you and take you to St. Paul."

Swiftly we glided on with our escort. The country had changed again. The river was narrow, and the shores low. It was a gentle, friendly river now, like a slow winding stream in some quiet French countryside. We could not see the peaceful farmhouses that lay beyond. But we could feel their presence.

I went to sleep, and wakened at dawn as the boat bumped dully. I looked out. We were at the wharf of St. Paul, with the skyscrapers of the great city silhouetted against the brightening horizon. Beyond, hidden by the bends of the river, lay Minneapolis. We had reached our goal.

I put on my dressing gown. Something heavy was in the pocket. I took it out. It was a fountain pen, covered with labels, and a tiny glass hole in the top where one might see Niagara Falls.

I went outside, and saw the wistful old man coming through the door of his cabin. I gave him the pen.

He blinked sleepily. "I must be getting kind of absent-minded," he said.

We walked on deck. Below us the roustabouts were hurrying, making the lines fast. Captain Buck stood near, smiling happily. Though the city was still asleep, stragglers were already hurrying down the bank to halt before the boat and gaze in awe.

The little man watched. His wistful face became ecstatic. "We're sure pioneers," he said.

XI

LOW WATER: ST. LOUIS TO NEW ORLEANS

Y OU won't get her through," said the fat visitor from the shore. "The water's too low. You'll get stuck on a sandbar sure and stay there the rest of the summer. River's the lowest it's been in forty years."

"We'll get her through," said Captain Dick.

We sat in the pilot house of the *Tennessee Belle* as she lay at the gray waterfront in St. Louis. It was strange to see the *Belle* in Missouri; her trade lay far to the South, between

Greenville in Mississippi and languorous New Orleans. Captain Dick Dicharry, her vivacious, quick-spoken owner, always left the steamboating of this region to his good friend Captain Buck of the *Golden Eagle,* whom I could see on the bow of that pleasant vessel a short distance down the bank, sitting in a canvas chair and smoking his early morning cigar. But Captain Dick had come to St. Louis to rent some barges and buy some machinery, and I was happy to catch him here at the wharf. For I was cub pilot on the vessel, and the *Belle* had long been my home.

The boat made ready to depart. The barges were lashed in place before the bow; some tattered roustabouts were dragging the shiny pieces of machinery aboard. St. Louis roustabouts sang little. But Captain Dick's negroes were New Orleans negroes, and as they toiled they chanted, in hushed melancholy:

> "Captain, Captain, change your mind,
> Take de cotton, but leave de seed behind."

The pilot, a pink-cheeked little man, blew a warning blast of the whistle.

The fat visitor made ready to go. "You'll get stuck on a bar sure," he repeated. "Maybe you could get the *Belle* through by herself. But you'll never do it with them barges loaded the way they are. They're drawing six and a half feet and ain't but five in the river plenty of places."

"We'll get her through," said Captain Dick.

The visitor disappeared up the bank.

In a moment the vessel began to move down the river. While the pink-cheeked pilot stood at the wheel, I sat on the bench with my tutor, the scholarly Captain Charley, who was the *Belle's* regular helmsman, and who would steer after we had reached Memphis. Together we watched the factories that lined the banks of Illinois and Missouri drift past and become smoky blurs on the horizon. Great rocks began to tower over us; below them showed long stretches of wooden piling, the dikes erected by the Government men to keep the river in its erratic channel. But the dikes were far out the water now; there were only long expanses of white sand and clay out of which the wooden poles rose like strange stockades set out on some troubled desert. The channel, far below them, was a mere muddy thread, marked by rows of red and black buoys, so narrow it seemed almost insufficient for a skiff to pass, much less a towboat loaded with its barges.

The pilot blew the whistle for soundings. Two negroes moved out to the end of the barges, and casting the lead began singing in rich, plaintive voices. "Quarter twain. Quarter less twain. Eight feet. Seven feet."

The boat with its long tow wound and twisted. Occasionally there was a dull grinding beneath us as the hull scraped the bottom of the river.

The pink-cheeked pilot looked at the sandy wastes stretching out like a great desert before him, then studied the burning, cloudless sky. It was nearing autumn. But the heat was the heat of mid-summer. "Hope we're going to get some rain," he declared. "If we don't pretty soon instead of steamboats on the river they'll have to be sending off to Africa for camels."

Uncle Jesse, the gentle-faced, withered old negro who served as the cabin boy, and had just arrived with the morning coffee, shook his snowy head. "Ain't going to be no rain, Captain. I seen that by that old yellow cat was a-sitting on the wharf in St. Louis. You can always tell if it's going to rain by looking at a cat's eyes. If they're all bright and shiny, the weather's going to be the same way. But if they got black spots in 'em, it's going to rain before another day. Way that there cat's eyes looked, it ain't going to rain before a year, maybe."

More massive rocks glided past us. There was a sudden change in the channel and a stony cliff loomed ahead. The vessel, caught in a swift current, sped toward it, and like a human weary of life seemed about to dash to its destruction. The pilot spun the wheel swiftly. The foremost barges gave a violent leap, and missed the towering wall by inches.

"Close one," said the pilot.

The vessel began weaving in and out the sandbars once more.

The day passed quickly, the boat halting and shivering like a patient in fever as it scraped a sandbar, while the leadsman at the bow chanted the calls in troubled rhythm. Flocks of ducks and geese floated over us, and rested on the water. Following at a long distance behind one flock, came a single goose flying in mournful solitude.

"He's a watchman goose done went to sleep," Uncle Jesse announced. "Gooses keeps watch when they're a-traveling just like they was men. Sometimes a watchman goose goes to sleep. And then they throws him out, and won't let him fly with them, or have a wife or nothing. Just has to go by himself thataway till he's dead."

Past St. Genevieve we drifted, where natives told how bold Jesse James swept down one day on a foray, and came in sight of Kaskaskia, that strange little settlement of Illinois, orphaned almost overnight when the river decided to shift its course, and left the land here separated from its parent state by all the width of the Mississippi.

We tied up along the willows soon after, for the channel, hazardous by day, had become impossible for night navigation.

A gaunt fisherman came over from a near-by shantyboat to request some medicine for his ill wife. Captain Dick found some drugs and added to them some delicacies from the table.

The shantyman's thin face lighted with gratitude. He looked off down the dark river. "Reckon you can't get the boat through, can you, Captain?" he murmured. "I was a-talking to the lightkeeper just before sundown, and he said they was a-tying up all the boats between here and Baton Rouge."

"We'll get her through," said Captain Dick.

We arose with the dawn. As the day advanced, it again grew hot, blistering, with the fiery sun drawing up more and more of the ever-shrivelling river.

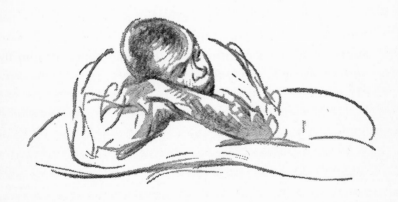

The smoke of Cape Girardeau showed ahead, once a thriving river town, its wharves crowded with long lines of chanting roustabouts; some miles beyond it lay Commerce Bar, scene of the great Mississippi lion hunt, where some city dwellers seeking excitement brought two lions from a circus and set out on their heroic safari, only to find the terrible beasts rubbing in friendliness against their tent, and pleading with their sad eyes for some of the fragrant hams and bacon hanging within.

"Funny things always going on around here," the pink-cheeked pilot chuckled. "I was coming down one time and I saw a tent back in the willows, with a big strapping fellow in a kind of ragged army uniform standing by it. Just as the boat was passing, a shot came out from somewhere and pretty near went through the pilot house. It happened twice, and the third time I got pretty mad, and took my pistol, and went to shore. But the fellow in the uniform came running up to meet me, and shook my hand. He wasn't shooting at me. He was just an old army sergeant that was living on the river, and he liked to salute the flag on any boat that was passing. He had what he called a saluting machine that was sure something to see. He'd blow a bugle, and a dog he had 'd jump up on a tree stump with a trap door in it like a trigger, and it made an American flag run up a little pole. A minute later a gun in a tree would go off like a cannon. And then the dog 'd sit up at attention till the flag came down."

We moved along the narrow channel, the boat, like a nervous, high-spirited horse, halting suspiciously as it neared a treacherous stretch of sand, backing in fright, then charging impetuously forward once more.

A heavy cloud of smoke appeared before us, and a moment

later the tops of some long bridges drifted into view. We were nearing Cairo, where the muddy Ohio sweeps down from its hills to join the Mississippi. In times of high water the little city was almost an island, with the two great rivers swirling angrily round its massive flood walls; now with the shrinking channel, the flood walls, high above the river bed, gave it the appearance of some medieval fortress set there to bar passage down the valley.

We decided to continue traveling during the night. Constantly when I waked for a moment with some unusual movement of the vessel, I could hear the negroes calling in their sad voices: "Quarter twain. Quarter less twain. Eight feet. Six and a half feet."

I arose early and looked out of my cabin. The river had changed violently, as though its junction with the Ohio had wrought some curious magic. The rocky cliffs, the brown dikes, the smoky cities were all vanished now; we were in a wilderness of swamp and sand, with white cranes flying in silvery arcs against the sky. Here and there the remnant of some broken levee showed starkly through the trees.

All day we drifted through the swampy solitudes. Past Reelfoot we glided, where hidden by the trees lay the mysterious lake formed by an earthquake, when a hole was suddenly opened in the earth, so vast, said the terror-struck natives, that the Mississippi flowed upstream until it was filled; past Caruthersville, where once ran the famous ferry called by rivermen "the hayburner," a tiny craft without steam and whose sole motive power was an amiable old horse lazily walking on a treadmill.

We neared a huge towboat, grounded on a sandbar, struggling to get free. We steamed by it, scraping the bottom constantly. We stopped at a tiny settlement in Tennessee. We were in the cotton country now; plantations were everywhere behind the levees. At the river a little tent show was playing, to share in the wages of the cotton pickers. Some shantyboats were moored at the bank. As we watched, a youth in overalls emerged from one of the floating structures, leading by the hand a sunbonneted old woman. Slowly they walked up the gangplank of the steamboat, and sought out Captain Dick. The old woman's face was a beautiful face, veined with delicate blue lines. But her eyes were red with weeping. Motionless she stood at the rail, while the youth spoke to Captain Dick quietly.

"My pappy was drowned three days ago a-running his fishing lines, Captain. And Mammy ain't a-feeling so good. We been a-looking for him everywhere, but he ain't come up yet. Some people says them's that's drowned comes up the fourth day, and some says the fifth. We took a bundle of corn shucks and put it on the river at night and lit it. People said it 'd sure go to where he was laying. But it didn't do no good, someways. We figured maybe he'd come up by your barges. Will you keep a-looking for him going down the river, Captain?"

Captain Dick nodded gently.

Night fell, and the boat glided down the river again. The stars shone brilliantly. A towboat appeared around a bend and blew a long blast of its whistle; the whistle of the *Belle* answered in deep melancholy.

On the deck the negro roustabouts were chanting again as they wheeled coal for the boilers:

> "Dis river is so deep and wide
> Can't git to my captain on de other side."

A new dawn came and Memphis was in sight now, its towering buildings piercing the hot sky. We landed, and I wandered along the wharf where the vessels of the famous Lee Line had anchored, crowded again with bales of cotton. I sauntered down Beale Street, with its negro barbecues, and saw the darkened windows of the hoodoo doctors, where spiders told fortunes by walking over a deck of cards, and women speaking outlandish tongues lighted the "three orphans," the three mysterious candles possessed of such dread power that when the final sputtering of the last candle was ended, the spelled victim in whose name it had been burned instantly fell dead.

I dined with friends, and afterward visited a negro church, filled with several hundred men and women, shouting and dancing, and leaping high in the air. Suddenly the exuberant devotions ceased. The ushers went about taking up the collection. The preacher, Brother Enoch, a giant negro with the soul of a Jeremiah, scolded his flock like a stern father his children, and counted the proceeds in indignation.

He threatened his disciples with a long skinny finger. "Ain't going to be no more services here till we git fifty-seven more cents," he boomed. "Some of you rich folks that always talks about what you're going to do for your preacher and this here church, you come up and give a quarter. And them of you as can't give a quarter give dimes. And them as can't give dimes give buffaloes and brownies."

The buffaloes and brownies dropped slowly into the basket. Brother Enoch opened a huge Bible and began to intone a sermon. His words rolled out like thunder.

It was time to return to the *Belle* now and I hurried down the hill to the water. A man in a derby hat, a lounger on the wharf boat, was talking in clipped accents to Captain Dick.

"Bet you five dollars you won't get her through, Captain," he asserted, spitting some tobacco over the side with abandon. "The gauge fell three tenths at Greenville last night, and there's four boats grounded near Shoofly, they said. And up on the Missouri, even the frogs is all tied up on the bank, the water's so low."

"Hand over your money," said Captain Dick.

I sat in the pilot house. In a few moments we were in the wilderness again, more desolate than before, with only the twinkling of the river lights to break the swampy blackness. An owl hooted in the distance; strange night birds drifted back and forth before the pilot house like restless ghosts seeking a haven.

We had left the pink-cheeked pilot at Memphis, and the scholarly Captain Charley was at the wheel now, smoking a cigar and talking his quiet philosophy. Apparently his thoughts and eyes were far from the water, but in some uncanny fashion, even though his back might be turned, the slightest change in the river or the shore brought an instant turn of the wheel. The foremost barge bumped along the edge of a sandbar which had suddenly developed within the buoys, and whined like a child in pain.

"Looks like Old Al is trying mighty hard to wrap us up in his tail," he murmured. "We could use a few cups of water out there. What does your cat say, Uncle Jesse?"

The old negro, who was pouring out the coffee, shook his head gravely. "I seen a other cat down at the wharf in Memphis," he answered. "Way his eyes was a shining there ain't going to be no more rain till Judgement Day." He set the coffeepot back on its wooden tray. "But I knowed a other cat once could tell more than rain. Was a cat on a boat where them ocean ships is, and the water's salty, and comes in and

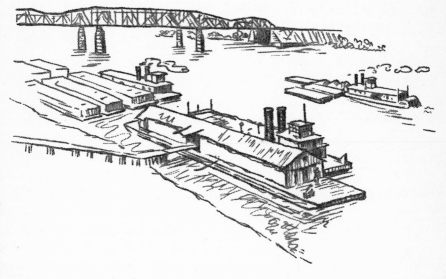

Memphis

goes out every day. If it was night, or foggy or anything, and the people couldn't see over the side, all they had to do was look at that cat's eyes. If his eyes was turned up, and had a black streak across 'em, the water was a-coming up stream mighty good. But if the streak was white, and his eyes was looking down, the water was running out to sea fast as it could go. A fellow come from way off in New York seen the cat, the captain told me, and wanted to give a thousand dollars for him. He wanted to buy it for the King of England, he said."

The sun was just rising as we passed Helena, with its medieval flood walls and gates like Cairo, and its streets where in a few hours the poor farmers from the near-by countryside would stroll with their wives through the streets, timidly looking into the store windows, or staring in awe at the loggers from the cypress swamps, with broad-brimmed hats like cowboys from the West.

We stopped at Greenville, rich little city of the Delta, proud of its millionaires and its culture. The hour was near midnight, but it was Saturday and the streets of the negro section were still teeming with black families come in from the plantations to spend their shares of a bale of cotton. Young colored bloods of the town sat on benches before the shabby poolrooms and barbershops, calling out to the sleek negresses who passed. Some distance away was a negro merry-go-round, its patrons not children, but grown men and women. Patiently they waited to get aboard the creaky vehicle, then as it halted, all dashed forward in an effort to climb aboard the battered lions, of which there were only four. The lucky quartet sat in ecstasy on their royal steeds, and waved to their less fortunate companions, compelled to content themselves with only a lean camel or a shaggy buffalo.

I returned to the boat. Greenville was the upper terminal of the *Belle's* regular run, and there were some barges waiting, with a towering cargo of cotton bales. We made them fast to the rest of our tow, and when the freight at the dock was aboard, steamed a short distance down the water. We halted as the glare of the searchlight showed a white mountain of cotton piled high on the bank.

The mate, who had come up to the pilot house, looked apprehensive. "You think we better take that cotton, Captain? It'll load her a foot deeper, maybe. Don't know with that extra foot whether we can make it to New Orleans."

"Load her," said Captain Dick.

In a moment a long line of black shining bodies was hurrying forward. Forming in pairs, they seized the huge bales with their cotton hooks, and chanting rhythmically, began rolling them down the hill. The task was difficult, for the bank was steep, and their feet slipped constantly. Suddenly a bale slid down the slope and sped toward the water.

"Look out! Old Al's going to git it!" shouted the roustabouts.

The negro from whom it had escaped charged down the bank in panic, trying to stop it with desperate stabs of his cotton hook. He succeeded at last, just as the great Juggernaut was about to take a final plunge into the water. He grinned with triumph.

We set off in the morning, the bow of the barges ahead white with flluffs of cotton, as though someone in the darkness had decorated them for a Christmas festival. The barges were deeper in the water now, and Captain Charley's eyes were watchful.

A girl wearing trousers appeared near the opposite shore, guiding an odd-shaped canoe whose motive power was a rickety paddle wheel propelled by her feet. She waved in excitement.

Captain Charley shook his head philosophically. "You can never tell what you're going to see on the river," he murmured. "It's like life. A grand circus and side show, with a different performance every minute. Just a little while ago a man started out from St. Louis to go all the way down the river in a wash tub. To make it float better he had an automobile inner tube tied around the edge. But he didn't get very far. A catfish or something ran into him. He got a flat tire, and didn't have a spare."

Twilight fell, and then darkness. Captain Charley puffed

at his cigar. "Bad place ahead," he said suddenly. He snapped on the searchlight. The white beam spread in a dazzling circle over the water. Above it, like a black mountain, showed the bank, wide, towering, with a swift current racing past. As we approached, a great section of the earthen wall caved and fell into the water. Some willows dropped onto the roof of the pilot house; the boat rocked heavily with the waves created by the avalanche. Ahead the buoys marking the changes of the channel executed a sharp right angle.

"Five and a half feet," called the shadowy leadsman on the starboard bow.

Captain Charley pulled a bell quickly. The vessel stopped in midstream, and with her wheel turning slowly in reverse, stood stationary.

"Bank must have caved and she hasn't dug out yet," he said. He pulled the bell again. The coughing of the smoke-stacks increased; the boat began to back slowly up the stream, then shifted its direction slightly, and moved down the water once more.

"Five and a half feet," repeated the leadsman on the starboard bow.

"Six feet," called the leadsman on the port.

The red glow of Captain Charley's cigar heightened. "Nothing to do but try it," he said.

The boat drifted slowly beneath the overhanging bank. More branches fell upon us. There was a smell of damp earth everywhere. Captain Charley whistled down the speaking tube to the engine room. "Give me all you've got, Doc," he said quietly.

The panting of the stacks became fevered. The violent churning of the paddle wheel shook the pilot house. There was a horrible grinding beneath the hull, and the great craft stood motionless.

The cigar in Captain Charley's mouth glowed brightly. He spun the wheel to its final extremity. The barges floundered an instant like wounded animals, then whined metallically, and went on their way.

Captain Charley snapped off the searchlight. "Old Al's tail pretty near got us," he said.

The lights of Vicksburg came into view. The boat made fast, and we climbed the steep hill that led to the town. It was late and the streets were deserted. Quietly we walked past the dignified old houses, sleeping like their inhabitants under canopies of widespreading trees. The moon was out, flooding the perfumed gardens with a magical light; it seemed as though this land had known only peace and restfulness, as though there had been no crackling rifles of the Union invaders, no booming cannon hurling destruction in the bitter siege of the War between the States.

We made our way to the boat again. When I awakened in the morning, we were moving slowly alongside a swamp, steamy, mysterious. Pendants of Spanish moss hung everywhere from the branches of the cypresses. Giant buzzards roosted in the twisting branches. Cranes stood gravely on rotting stumps, like ghostly sentinels. We seemed lost in some distant land of the Amazon or the Orinoco.

Captain Dick grew thoughtful. "Queer country in here. No wonder the roustabouts don't like it. River pirates used to hide back in the cypresses and kill everybody on the rafts coming down. They say there was one family of pirates lived on a shantyboat had a beautiful daughter that looked like an angel. She'd get a riverman on her shantyboat, and be pretending to look for a drink of whisky or water or something, when her father and brother would come up behind. And there'd be another riverman sink to the bottom. They say pretty funny things still go on in there sometimes."

Uncle Jesse looked out at the moss-hung trees and shuddered. "There's plenty of things a-going on. I know a nigger fisherman, Hot Mouth, they calls him, went in there to find him some herbs when he had a fever, and he said he got lost and seen things was half man and half pig. He come on 'em sudden, a little ways off, and they was standing around, laughing and talking like they was men. And so he went up to 'em, and started to ask 'em whichaway to go. They turned and looked at him. And jest like lightning they dropped to the ground and come running after him on four feet. And he seen they wasn't men at all, but hogs, with two big teeth in 'em like them iron claw things people carries ice with. He got away from 'em all right. But they cut his legs mighty bad. He's done showed me the scars plenty of times up in the barbershop at Vicksburg."

The swamps continued endlessly.

There was a pronounced change in the weather now. As the morning advanced the sky began to be streaked with long ribbons of cloud that lay like gray rainbows across the horizon.

Captain Charley studied them, and puffed his cigar. "Looks like the dry spell's going to break," he said. "Going to have a good storm tomorrow."

Captain Dick nodded. "She'll be a mighty good storm."

The clouds grew heavier, piling up in somber black masses, reflected shadowily in the yellow water of the river.

The bluffs of Natchez came in sight. We docked at Natchez under the Hill.

When I returned to the boat after dinner, the clouds in the sky were thickening, and the air was growing heavy, humid. As we set off down the water, lightning began to flash in the distance. Captain Charley looked at the barometer. But though the sky was thus charged with promise, there was no change in the level of the shallow water before us. The leadsmen took their endless soundings; the vessel crept along hesitantly, like an old blind man feeling his way.

All night the lightning flashed intermittently, continuing while the vessel stopped at a plantation in the wilderness to load more cotton. The lightning ceased with the rising of the sun. The clouds were changed now, taking curious shapes like unfolding black fans carried by slaves in some funeral procession. Sudden gusts of wind blew shrilly through the black cypresses, then died as quickly as they had begun. Cranes flew before the pilot house in troubled flight as though uncertain of their course.

A gaunt figure rowed out from a shantyboat to bring us some catfish. One by one he lifted the gleaming shapes lying in the flooded bottom of his craft and tossed them onto the deck where the black cook stood waiting. "Going to have a bad storm," he called. "I just been hunting, and the rabbits is deep in their holes."

We glided past the penitentiary at Angola, with its block houses set alongside the river where guards watched every

passing log to see that it sheltered no fleeing convict; saw opposite it the twisting mouth of Old River, leading off to the strange waste lands of the Red and the Atchafalaya, where grim malaria lurked in the shadows of the cypresses, and strange men wandered with prices on their heads.

Night fell. Masses of cloud spun and twisted overhead, like the smoky spirals whirling up from the stacks. The stars twinkled with a too bright luster, suddenly vanishing when a long black shadow reached out toward them, as though it were a great arm extinguishing a candle. Lightning began flashing again, in streaks of vivid yellow and red. The air grew damp, soggy, like bread left a long time in the rain.

We sat in the pilot house drinking coffee.

The last star vanished. The sky became a smoky, tossing waste.

Captain Charley constantly watched the barometer. "Falling fast," he declared at length. "Guess I'd better tie her up. Don't want to get caught out in the middle of the river."

The boat headed to the shore.

Suddenly a huge cloud, like the smoke arising from an oil fire, appeared on the horizon.

The cigar in Captain Charley's lips grew rigid an instant. "She's coming," he said quietly. "Ahead of time. I think she'll get us."

He called down the tube to the engine room. The stacks began to cough fiercely. The paddle wheel sped faster.

Blackness swept down upon us. There came a roar like that of a thousand rushing trains. The darkness was rent by a blinding flash of lightning. Rain began to beat a fierce tattoo against the windows.

Captain Charley spun the wheel. But the boat obeyed him only feebly as it swept along in the fierce wind. The pilot house trembled; the guy wires lashing it to the deck sang shrilly. A shantyboat swept past, torn from its moorings, with a woman and some ragged children silhouetted for an instant against the windows. Logs thundered deafeningly against the bow.

The wind took a new direction and began to drive the vessel to the shore. A dredge moored along the bank loomed before us, dark, ominous, the rain coursing in sheets from the topmost deck. Captain Charley spun the wheel vainly. Closer and closer we sped toward the huge, menacing shadow. Captain Charley jerked the backing bell. The boat hesitated, then swung away. The dredge vanished.

A swamp showed along the shore, the lower part of the gnarled cypresses submerged in the black water. As the wind lulled for an instant, the pilot drove the vessel forward; with uncanny skill he guided it between the streaming trunks, so close the upper branches scraped the pilot house. The mate barked a command. Half a dozen negroes carrying a heavy line leaped into the murky water. In a moment the vessel was fast, locked in a forest vise.

The wind rose again to a fury. Now and then there came an explosive crackling as a great tree in the distance crashed to the ground. We waited, smoking, and talking quietly.

The storm ended; the black masses of cloud swept off to the horizon. The air grew cool, fragrant. The stars shone brilliantly once more. In a farmyard hidden behind the willows a pig grunted cheerfully. The roustabouts splashed into the water once more to loosen the lines. The vessel left its forest haven.

We went on taking soundings, though water was rushing over the sandbars in torrents. Then a dull glow appeared above the black lines of trees before us, soon becoming a string of lights along the shore.

Captain Dick drank some coffee and sighed in relief. "It's Baton Rouge," he declared. "We're in deep water."

Past the city with its huge oil docks and its towering State Capitol we drifted. We were out of the swamps now, in the rich sugar coast of Louisiana. Levees hemmed us tightly on both sides; beyond them we could see the tops of the houses and the little churches of the friendly French inhabitants. This was the land of the Cajuns. Past Plaquemine with its lock that lifted vessels across the levee to the gentle flowing bayous of Evangeline, we drifted while I slept, past Donaldsonville surrounded by its rustling fields of sugar cane. Several times I awakened as the passing of some ocean vessel set the boat to rocking violently.

In the morning, the river described a long crescent; the skyline of a great city showed ahead. We had arrived at New Orleans, metropolis of the Mississippi, city of octoroons and pralines, of slave markets and scandals, of Marseilles and Mardi Gras.

We neared the docks, where long ocean freighters lay waiting. There was a stir below as the roustabouts began lifting the tarpaulins from the cotton. Sadly they chanted as they pulled at the heavy canvasses:

> "Captain, Captain, change your mind,
> Take de cotton, but leave de seed behind."

Uncle Jesse emptied the water cooler in the pilot house. "About them cats," he said. "I knowed a cat was owned by a fellow on Canal Street could tell the weather better than any of 'em. He had a mouth all full of gold teeth, jest like a man.

When the weather was a-going to be good, he'd kind of hold his mouth open and you could see the gold teeth a-shining like a lantern. But when it was going to be bad, he'd keep it shut like it was locked with iron. If you made him open it, you'd see the teeth was black as the soot in a stove."

The chanting negroes cast the lines ashore. The boat touched the wharf gently.

"We got her through," said Captain Dick.

Boats at New Orleans

XII

RIVER'S END

A DEEP fog lay over the New Orleans waterfront, almost hiding from my view the *Tennessee Belle* down whose gangplank I had just come hurrying. The great docks rose out of the mist like gloomy prisons of the ancient Spanish days where mute captives lay dying in their chains; the steamy streets, heavy with the smell of spice and rotting hemp, were deserted. A switch engine moved like a ghost up and down its gleaming tracks, coughing out funereal clouds of smoke that instantly mixed with the gray fog and made the

air acrid, impenetrable. At times the whistle would blow
mournfully and the train would come to a sharp halt; there
would follow a series of dull rumblings, like distant thunder,
as one after another the freight cars bumped together. A
shrouded figure, skulking in the shadow of the wharves,
shuffled off as the dock watchman approached silently. The
mist thickened.

The watchman, a drawling Mississippian, chewed his tobacco gravely as I waited for the cab that was to take me to
another section of the harbor.

"You going down to the Jetties?" he asked.

I nodded, and told him that all my life I had wanted to
look at the Mississippi where it flows into the sea.

He gave an answering nod of comprehension. "I'd like to
see it, too. But you better look out for that country down
there. Mighty funny people in them bayous and islands, they
says. I thought French talking people was funny, but these
here people talks something ain't like no talking you ever
heard. And the place is full of smugglers, and opium, and
Chinamen, they says." He took a new chew of tobacco.
"That's where they smuggles all the Chinamen that gets into
the country. If you go out with the shanty people down there,
you better take your gun."

A taxicab came out of the fog. I climbed inside. Along the
wharves we rode, past dim ships creaking at their moorings,
or blowing their foghorns eerily in the steamy veil obliterat-
ing the earth and the water.

"That's mighty funny country down there between New
Orleans and the Gulf," said the cab driver. "You better look
out for it. They says there's killers hiding from the law down
there 'd murder their own mothers for a nickel. Used to be
the pirates hid in the swamps, but these fellows is worse. It's

them that smuggles the Chinamen. When they're a-doing the smuggling, and the law comes after 'em, they throw all the Chinamen in the water to drown. If you're going down there, you better take your gun."

The cab stopped in front of a wharf. Before me a spectral roustabout was rolling endless barrels down into a long black hole; beyond misty ships were groping their way, like great animals suddenly stricken with blindness. I followed the roustabout along the gangway. A boat was anchored at the water's edge, a shadowy little Diesel boat where figures in raincoats moved vaguely. I stepped onto the creaky plank connecting it with the shore. That step was as though I were a giant with huge boots made for striding across the spaces of the universe; I had suddenly stepped upon another star.

To me the Mississippi had always been America in its most typical, its most native expression. It had meant negroes toiling in fields of cotton and rustling sugar cane. It had meant the drawling bottom farmers of Missouri and Arkansas, and the blue-eyed shantymen drifted down from the Kentucky hills. But when I walked aboard this boat I was met by a riverman whose voice and manner were far from Missouri, and to whom my Kentucky speech was as a foreign tongue. For the crew of this boat, and the crews of all the boats in the country of the Jetties to which I was departing, and many of the shore dwellers as well, came out of a country so different from the Mississippi as to approach the realm of fantasy. They were Jugo-Slavians.

The boat gave a feeble toot, and with a wheeze of its engine, set off blindly into the mist. The fog began to drift before us, in long, twisting columns, like giant trees in a storm. Beyond them the faint lights of New Orleans flickered and faded, like will-o'-the-wisps in a distant swamp. Ships drifted mysteriously past us, their bells clanging steadily, like rattlesnakes warning any passers to beware.

The captain, a thoughtful, dignified figure, came forward to meet me, and led me down to the cabin where half a dozen men were eating, and talking in their thick Slavic language that I could not understand. They were dark men, with long black hair, and flashing black eyes. But their faces were friendly.

I sat down at the table, and made ready to eat. With the experience of a foolish, mossless life spent in travel in distant places I looked with suspicion at the drinking glass set near my plate. It was a rough little boat, and water would be a problem, I reflected. Unobserved I took out the iodine pencil I always carried for such emergencies and prepared to put a few drops in the tumbler.

"Dreenk, dreenk, my friend," boomed the mate, a swarthy giant beside me, as he filled my glass to overflowing from a great pitcher.

I drank. I had no need of my iodine pencil, for there was no water problem. There was no water. On the table there was only wine, the same rich Jugoslav wine I had drunk when I sat in the café at the station in Belgrade, awaiting my train for Istanbul.

I finished and went outside to watch the fog. The trees of mist were changing now and becoming great spectral animals like elephants and dinosaurs, marching in slow procession past us; between their legs and trunks occasionally there came the flash of a light on shore, like the lantern of some phantom hunter.

The engine of the boat creaked and whined dismally.

A ghostly little vessel without lights glided silently past us and disappeared in the darkness.

A stunted little negro wearing an overseas cap, who stood on the bow near me, watched the vanishing vessel and shuddered. "That's one of them boats going out to smuggle the Chinamen," he murmured. "This here's the kind of night they go, when the law can't follow 'em. They meet the big ocean ships a-coming from Cuba out in the Gulf, and git the Chinamen there. I know a nigger worked on one of them boats and he said they don't carry nothing but whisky and some big stones, the stones to tie to the legs of the Chinamen so they never come up when they throw 'em in the water, and the whisky to drink so they can forget they killed 'em. The river here's full of ha'nts. And pretty near all of 'em's got slant eyes."

A smaller boat, a fishing craft, drifted past us, and another, so close they almost touched our sides. On their dim-lit decks I could see swarthy men like the crew of the vessel on which

I was standing; they called out to our captain in Jugo-Slav.

Mosquitoes began to assail us fiercely. I went inside, but there was no relief. The insects crawled through the holes of the screens. A heavy perfume swept over the water, the fragrance of the unseen orange groves along the banks. A little wharf showed vaguely through the mist. The boat halted to put off some supplies. From the darkness came thick Jugo-Slav voices once more.

We set off again through the fog.

I stood at the prow with Nikola, the giant mate, and talking of the gaitered peasants that walked the streets of the little towns in what was once Serbia, listened to him tell how this strange colony had been born here on the Mississippi.

Some years after the Civil War, a Dalmatian fisherman, weary of his beautiful but troubled land, came to America and chanced upon the region where we were now travelling. So cursed was the country with the mosquitoes now torturing us, so hostile was it in every way to humanity, that no one would remain except the wandering hunter or the hardiest Cajun. But the newly arrived fisherman was accustomed to hostility and difficulty. Day and night he worked without resting. Oysters and shrimp were plentiful, and after a time his long empty pockets were filled with money. Other Dalmatian men came to join him. Soon their wives followed, and their children, and then pretty girls for their sons to marry. They all thrived in the new country, for they were all expert fishermen, and knew the ways of the water. And some of them began settling on the shore, where they could grow the oranges we were smelling, and ferment the fragrant orange wine. They were a gay, a happy people, and they brought their gaiety with them, and their legends, and their superstitions. And to the rare whites and negroes who lived along the banks, they became known simply as the "Austrians."

The fog thickened. All traces of the shore and the water vanished. The world was an endless white curtain ever parting to let us pass. A boat without lights darted suddenly before us, barely missing our prow, and vanished.

The little negro watched uneasily. "Hope we don't hit none of them smuggler boats. They git a nigger on them smuggler boats and they work him till you can count the bones in him, jest like the strings on a old guitar. Then they kill him like the Chinamen. If we git back to New Orleans, I sure ain't coming down here no more."

I went to sleep, with the distant foghorns blowing a troubled symphony.

I awakened in the morning, with the boat still moving steadily down the stream. The fog had vanished. The world had changed once more. Everywhere as far as the eye could see lay desolate green marshes, so low they seemed on a level with the water. The air was softer now, and touched with the sea. Flocks of cranes and pelicans flew silently overhead; two porpoises rolled and tumbled as in escort before us.

A fishing boat neared us, and the pilot blew the whistle sharply. The porpoises ahead of the boat seemed to leap out of the water as in response.

The pilot, Janko, a fat jolly little man, thrust his bald head out of the tiny box-like pilot house, so that he much resembled a figure in a Punch and Judy show. He pointed to the porpoises, and laughed in delight. "Every time I blow the whistle they will jump this way," he assured me in heavy Slavic accents. "They love the whistle so. They are like children with the whistle."

The giant mate, Nikola, standing near by, nodded in

affirmation. "They are fine animals, the porpoise, not like the shark or the optopuss which kill men. The porpoise is man's friend. If a man's body is in the sea, always the porpoise will carry it into shore, so that he may be found by his family and given a fine burial by the priest. So it was at Dubrovnik in Dalmatia when I was a boy. So is it here."

The fat Janko spun the wheel to swing the vessel around some low dikes projecting like a fence into the water. "Once I saw the porpoise do this thing. It was at Burwood, where the Government people stay who build the Jetties. A man had drowned working there and been washed out to the sea. Five days they searched for him. Then one morning, just as the sun was rising in the sky, I saw two porpoises, swimming. They were holding up out of the water a body, the body of the man who had been drowned. And behind them were twenty other porpoises, swimming so slowly, like men walk in a church when people have died. Yes, the porpoise is the friend of man."

Nikola lit a cigarette that was filled with a black European tobacco and set it in his heavy-jowled face. "He must be the friend of man. Because he was once himself a man. He was once a sailor on a sailing ship in the old days on the Red Sea. He was a very bad man, who had killed many other men on the ship, and one day, very angry, the captain threw him into the water that he might die. But as he was drowning, he prayed to his God and his God took pity upon him and turned him into a porpoise. Now he never takes a life. Never even does he fight. Always does he try to make peace, and to save. This my father told me in Dubrovnik. And this is so."

A Government boat passed and a lanky figure standing at the rail waved and called out in a voice bearing the unmistakable mark of Texas. "Howdy, Nick!" he shouted. "How's tricks?"

The great Jugo-Slav beamed upon him. "OK! OK!" he called in excitement.

It was time for breakfast now, and I went below to eat. The food on the boat was as strange as its legends. The cook was a negro, and those who ate his cooking Slavs; the result was a mixture of Belgrade and Memphis beyond human power to classify. There were fried potatoes prepared in a fashion one instant savoring of a tiny inn in Serajevo, the next recalling Bill's Bar-B-Q along a highway in Arkansas.

I went outside again. A great man-of-war bird sailed over us, its giant black wings outstretched against the sky, like a huge noiseless airplane. Everywhere were pelicans, standing in rows, sometimes so close together that once I thought their legs in the distance were the posts of some odd Government dike. The river was high for the summer. But here a flood from up the river was not feared by the inhabitants, for the water was diffused through so many mouths. The dreaded flood was the flood that came upstream, a great tidal wave that swept in with a hurricane from the Gulf. When the Jugo-Slav natives received news of the coming of one of these inundations it was a legend that they said to each other: "Save the wine first. The people can wait." And they hastened to carry the casks of their beloved red wine away from the water's ravages.

I went below where the negro roustabouts were working, preparing the freight for the next landing. They were quiet, repressed negroes, lacking the gaiety of their fellows up the river.

The blue sky darkened, and a sudden storm swept over the water. The boat rocked heavily. Squalls of rain beat down upon us. The boat seemed to be moving through sheets of liquid glass. Lightning flashed intermittently; thunder rolled dully over the marshes. A great man-of-war bird flew swiftly past us, so low I could plainly see the structure of its wings.

There was a blinding flash of lightning and an explosive clap of thunder that set the boat to quivering.

The cook, a massive round-faced negro wearing a green turban that gave him the air of a Mohammedan returned from Mecca, shook his head. "This ain't a natural river down here," he murmured. "The birds ain't natural. The water ain't natural. And the storms ain't natural, neither."

The thunder continued to crash deafeningly. The engine creaked dolefully. The boat floundered onward.

The cook watched a negro shooting dice who before each play was carefully touching something concealed in the pocket of his tattered coat. "I don't know why I cooks on this boat. This here kind of boat ain't no kind of boat for a black man. Even the hoodoos around here ain't natural. I ain't saying nothing about the hoodoos like that nigger's got so he can win at crap shooting. But people round here does hoodooing ain't like any hoodooing I ever knowed. Like the time that fellow was on the boat come out with a big shotgun."

Nikola stuffed a piece of wood into a crack over a window through which a stream of water was gushing. His face grew grave. "He means the time the man shot his work. But this is not what you call hoodooing." He puffed at his black cigarette. "It was a man on this boat who was a loafer, a good for nothing. I do not know why the captain keeps him. And one day he comes out of the cabin carrying a great shotgun. 'Who is it that you are going to kill?' I ask him. 'I am going to kill my work,' he answers. 'I am too tired of working.'

And he goes up on the deck, and he says some strange words, and the gun shoots like a great cannon into the sky. And I know then that he will do no more work, for I had a brother in my own country was a loafer also, and he went out and shot his work, and after that he would do nothing. Only would he lay in the bed all the day. And that is the way it was with this one. All the day now he stays in a little place up the river where the shrimp fishermen come and sits and plays the guitar and sings. But this is no hoodooing, my friend. This is so."

There was a momentary lull in the storm, and putting on my raincoat, I walked to the prow to watch the dashing waves. The roustabouts moved silently near me, making the tarpaulins secure. Spray stung my face. It was not the spray of the river; it was sharp, salty.

An oyster boat with no life visible anywhere scudded past. "It's one of them smuggler boats," murmured the dwarfish negro with whom I had been talking during the night. "Them smugglers never let you see their faces. They looks jest like oyster boats. But when you open up the bottom, there's twenty Chinamen laying there, packed like tomatoes in a can. And if you open up the oysters they got in the barrels, they're full of this here sticky stuff they calls Chinese tobacco, puts you to sleep for twenty years, they says. The swamps is all full of that Chinese tobacco, buried in big holes."

The wind increased to a fierce gale that forced us inside the cabin. The boat danced over the waves, like a runner leaping an endless line of hurdles. Water streamed in torrents everywhere; each board, each rope was a gushing Niagara.

The turbaned cook went off and returned looking worried. "Captain says he's going all the way to the Gulf today," he mumbled. "Fine day to be a-going there. I can't figure out these funny-talking people. They won't tie up a boat noways. Look at them waves. They're jumping over the pilot house, and we ain't nowheres near there yet. If I'd have knowed he was going to the Gulf, I'd have sure stayed in New Orleans."

The storm lulled again.

The boat stopped at a shabby wharf where a few fishing craft were anchored; the roustabouts began to carry ashore some flour. From the fishermen I learned some of the mysteries of the river here; how one night the catch will be strange fish from the deep sea, and the next morning in the same ten feet of water it will be the buffalo and the yellow cat of the Mississippi. I learned how the fish were the truest of all weather prophets. When the fisherman could catch nothing, he knew that a bad storm was coming; the fish had been warned long ahead, and had swum far out to sea so that the great waves would not dash them ashore. I heard the troubles of the oystermen; how the oysters in many ways are like humans. When the water becomes stagnant, they grow sick with fever and die, for an oyster catches fever from water as easily as a delicate child. I heard how the great schools of drumfish rush into the seed beds the oyster men have prepared after weeks of labor, and when they have attached themselves firmly to the shells, suck out every oyster with a loud noise like the beating of a drum.

A sad young man, with the typical high-cheekboned face of some regions of the Balkans, was hammering at a curious fish box.

Janko, the fat pilot, called to him jovially. "What you do there, Stefan? Do you build your own coffin? To be an oysterman you might as well be dead."

The fisherman shrugged his shoulders. Soon after he moved up the wharf.

Janko watched him go, thoughtful now. "It is bad to be an oysterman. I know because I myself have been one. It is work, work, all the time. Each night you are so tired you are asleep before you are in your bed. Look at Stefan. Eight years has he been an oysterman, and each day he passes Burwood, where he can go to the picture show. But he does not go. Why? Because he is an oysterman. He knows only his oysters. So tired is he always that when the sun is shining, he thinks it is night, and when it is raining he will talk of how bright is the sun. No, it is not good to be an oysterman."

The boat glided from the wharf and down the river once more. The water was losing the coffee color so typical of the Mississippi and was becoming a dull gray. The flocks of pelicans increased and the great man-of-war birds drifted constantly overhead. Even the river markers were different than those up the valley, queer frames like black crucifixes raised in supplication out of this desolate land. Often on their wooden arms a man-of-war bird and a pelican would stand side by side, like solemn sentinels. Occasionally a cow belonging to some lightkeeper appeared on the bank. But it was a lean, unhappy cow, too dejected even to moo or raise its head as the boat sputtered on its way. We passed a great ocean liner coming up the stream; soon another floated by us, going down. We rocked in its wake.

We caught a flashing glimpse of some animal darting through the marshes.

"It's a otter," said the little negro. "A otter's the smartest animal there is. A dog can chase him all day, and then you can go and find him right where he started, sitting up and licking his paws so the dog can't track him no more."

There was a new flurry of rain and the wind blew shrilly again. The wind and rain suddenly ceased. The clouds overhead changed, and began piling up in white fleecy mountains, the beautiful clouds of the Gulf.

We stopped at a landing where a boat was waiting, the boat of the Government Biological Survey, and put ashore some groceries for the bronzed youths who were trying to unriddle the secrets of the marshes. A great ocean freighter showed ahead, and on the bank beyond it two low frame buildings stood on piles over the water. Half a dozen little boats with iron handlebars fixed to the top were moored a short distance away. A man carrying a suitcase emerged from the nearest building, and stepping aboard one of the odd little craft, headed out toward the freighter. We had reached Pilot-town, near the Head of the Passes. The Mississippi was making ready to join the sea.

It was a melancholy place, this Pilot-town, like an outpost far up some jungle river in Africa; the pilots themselves seemed sad men, weighed down by the loneliness of the green wastes on every side. There were two groups of steersmen here; one the river pilots who took the ships to New Orleans, the other the bar pilots who steered the vessels through the mouth and beyond the shoals to the Gulf.

We steamed on under a brilliant sky. The water was almost green now, with the current so mild we seemed to be traveling over the surface of a glassy lake. Then the shore before us broke, and the channel divided sharply. Wide gray arms of water still fringed by the endless green marshes stretched before us into the distance. We were at the Head of the Passes, where the ships that sail to the West and the East take their separate ways.

We chose the pass that led to the Westward.

The porpoises had increased to a whole school now, bounding and dancing; the man-of-war birds floated over them in slow, black circles like gigantic buzzards waiting for their dying prey.

The turbaned cook watched the porpoises as he peeled the potatoes for supper. "It ain't a natural river. A river's a river with catfish in her. Not these here kind of things. You put a line in here and you don't know what you're getting. One day I was a-fishing here and I seen a fish come up a-holding a big sword that was all on fire, jest like he was a angel in the Bible. And a other time I seen six fish come out of the water and fly, jest like they was birds. They flew all over them bushes on the bank for a couple of minutes like they was a-looking for something they wanted to eat, and when they didn't find nothing, they flew back into the water again. People says them flying fish is the worst things was ever in the water. Says they'll eat the blood right out of you."

Nikola who was beside me, grunted, and sucked angrily at his cigarette. "There is nothing in the sea so bad as the optopuss at Dubrovnik. Nothing is so bad as the optopuss."

The Gulf began to be visible, a vivid blue under the blazing tropical sun. The flat shores along which we were coursing seemed to sink even closer to the water now, and grew always narrower, till we appeared to be traveling between two thin ribbons of green sod laid there by some foolish gardener. Everywhere were long rows of wooden pilings, as though the gardener were dubious of his experiment, and had set out these supports to keep the grassy ribbons from dissolving into the sea.

A little settlement came in sight, a bleak pile of bare frame dwellings, with here and there a larger structure rising out of the rest. This was Burwood, the last outpost in the marshy wilderness, the headquarters of the Army Engineers. Here they watched from day to day the constant battle between the river and the sea, while the river slowly laid down the rich earth of Ohio and Wisconsin and Nebraska, and built its shores further and further into the Gulf.

They were a kindly people, like engineers everywhere, with a generous welcome for the stranger. But it was a sad little settlement, its boardwalks ending after a few hundred yards in swamps steaming with mosquitoes. Its inhabitants possessed an air of permanent melancholy, like the homesick Englishmen I had known at desolate stations far off in Arabia.

We went on our way. The green ribbons that faced the shore were mere threads now, tenuously separating the river from the waters of the Gulf everywhere around us. A solitary building high on poles showed ahead. It was the Advanced Pilot Station, where the steersmen waited for the ocean vessels, and went out to bring them over the shoals. On both sides of it stretched low green mounds; we had come at last to the Jetties. The gray water beneath us still bore here and there a faint touch of yellow as though the Mississippi, stubborn, reluctant, fought against final dissolution; but on the other side of the thin dikes enclosing us, there was everywhere the brilliant blue of the Gulf. This was the River's End.

We sat awhile at the pilot station, gazing at the far horizon, where the masts of a wrecked ship rose starkly. The air was pure salt now, and tropical. A man climbed up from a pilot craft, carrying an enormous bunch of bananas, the gift of the captain of some banana boat. We put the last case of evaporated milk on the shabby pier, and started up the river.

The sun set soon after, and a heavy fog swept over the water once more. The shores vanished. The boat sped on through a lost world. Occasionally a great misty shape rose up before us, and floated off with a ghostly flapping of wings.

A cry drifted out of the darkness, prolonged, dismal.

The dwarfish negro listened intently. "It's a fox," he said at length. "He's found one of them dead Chinamen. They always barks that way when they finds a Chinaman."

The foggy air grew hot, stifling. Clouds of mosquitoes swept across the deck, like new waves of the enveloping mist. They stung me till one eye was closed; with the other I could only see through a faint crack between the swollen lids. I held the lids open with my finger.

We were moving close to the bank now. Curious rustlings came from the hidden bushes; whether they were animal or human I could not tell. In the distance an owl hooted forlornly.

The boat steamed on slowly, feeling its way.

We halted at a fish dock appearing suddenly through the mist. We were back in Jugo-Slavia now. Some Jugoslavian men and women with their children trooped merrily aboard, bound to New Orleans for a holiday.

Lights showed faintly ahead and we stopped at a little

Slavic settlement on the bank. I climbed up a marshy trail with Nikola and stumbled through the fog to a tiny café. The room was crowded with a noisy throng, talking the explosive languages of the Balkans. Men stood at the scarred bar drinking huge glasses of golden wine, and gesticulating in excitement. At one end a man was singing in a clear sweet voice a song of the Adriatic. I listened, though the mosquitoes were stinging my ankles till they seemed to be seared with fire. Through it all a nickel phonograph kept up a thunder of raucous swing tunes.

We strolled back through the fog to the boat and resumed our journey. The heavy fragrance of the unseen orange groves along the shore again touched the water. On the fog-swept deck the Jugo-Slavs talked and sang their merry songs. I went to sleep with their voices ringing in my ears.

I awoke early in the morning with the gray wharves of the New Orleans Dock Board everywhere around us. I washed hastily and made ready to land.

Nikola strode over to bid me good-by. "You will come again," he said. "Then maybe, when they blow the whistle you will see the mama and papa porpoise play with their baby and throw him up in the air like a child, and catch him so careful when he comes down. I have seen it many times off Dubrovnik. It is a very pretty thing to see."

I went onto the shore.

A taxi drove up, and whirling me through the crowded streets, brought me to a hotel, bustling with activity. Over the desk was a sign lettered in gold: "Kiwanis Meets Here Every Tuesday."

The clerk handed me the pen to register.

"Do you want your room with or without air conditioning?" he asked.

I was back in America.

The elevator carried me quickly to my room. Looking out the window, I could see the river spread out far below me, the crescent harbor of New Orleans with its towboats and tug boats and great ocean freighters moving slowly into their docks. I looked toward the south, which I had just left behind me, with its orange groves, and its porpoises, and its floods that come upstream, then toward the north where lay cotton-fringed Memphis and mellow St. Louis and the bustling twin cities of Minneapolis and St. Paul.

The whole sweeping panorama of the river unrolled before me. I saw again the blue Gulf with its man-of war birds and its pelicans. I saw again the mysterious cypress swamps of Louisiana and Mississippi and the dazzling white sandbars of Arkansas. I saw the low green hills of Tennessee and Kentucky and Illinois and Missouri, and the towering Palisades of Iowa and Wisconsin. I saw Lake Pepin with its storms and its strange legends, and the limpid river that flows so gently through the Minnesota countryside beyond. I saw the pilots at their wheels, and the shantymen with their nets and their catfish, and the roustabouts chanting as they carried their great bales of cotton. I saw the towboat-men, hauling at the lines of their huge barges, and the show-boatmen drifting on their happy way from town to town. I saw the engineers with their snag boats and their survey boats and their levees twisting like yellow serpents along the banks. And I saw the lightkeepers braving storm and flood to light their lamps, that their fellow rivermen might safely pass.

I thought of the vastness of the river, which divides the nation, yet unites it. And I thought of the other great rivers of the world: the Tigris with its curious rounded boats, like floating baskets, the Ganges with its burning ghats, and the Nile with its Pyramids.

And I reflected how it is little wonder that men in the ancient times built temples to their rivers. For where there is no river with its cooling waters there is only desert, with burning sands and dust and death. Where there is a river there is beauty—and life.

And as the river dweller stands in his boat at twilight, watching the birds fly against the fading sky, and listening to the lapping of the water against the prow and the soft murmur of the wind in the reeds, he knows that he is one of the blessed of the universe. For he has communed with the gods.